THE CHURCH AND THE HUMAN QUEST FOR TRUTH

INTRODUCTIONS TO CATHOLIC DOCTRINE

This series provides readable scholarly introductions to key themes in Catholic doctrine, written by preeminent scholars from around the world. The volumes of the series are suitable for college, university, and seminary courses, as well as for educated readers of all ages who seek to grow in their understanding of the Catholic faith.

■ ■ ■

PUBLISHED VOLUMES

Avery Cardinal Dulles, S.J., *Magisterium, Teacher and Guardian of the Faith*
Daniel A. Keating, *Deification and Grace*
Steven A. Long, *The Teleological Grammar of the Moral Act*
Charles Morerod, O.P., *The Church and the Human Quest for Truth*

FUTURE VOLUMES

Kenneth Whitehead, *Vatican II*
Guy Mansini, O.S.B., *Priesthood*
Edward T. Oakes, S.J., *Jesus Christ*
John Yocum, *The Sacraments*

THE CHURCH AND THE HUMAN QUEST FOR TRUTH

■ ■ ■

CHARLES MOREROD, O.P.

Sapientia Press
of Ave Maria University

Sapientia Press
of Ave Maria University
5050 Ave Maria Blvd.
Ave Maria, FL 34142
888-343-8607

Cover Design: Eloise Anagnost

Cover Image: Master Legend, St. Priest. *Life of Saint Peter: Jesus handing the keys to Saint Peter.* Oil (around 1470) 89 × 120 cm. Wallraf-Richartz-Museum—Fondation Corboud, Cologne, Germany.

Photo Credit: Erich Lessing/Art Resource, NY

Printed in the United States of America.

Library of Congress Control Number: 2007928360

ISBN-13: 978-1-932589-43-6

TABLE OF CONTENTS

INTRODUCTION

WHAT DOES the Church have to do with our human life? Is it simply one of these many organizations that provide some services for people still interested in religion?

The Church is actually more than that. She is the gift thanks to which we can fully and happily develop who we are.

Every human being wants to be happy. At the very heart of our life is some desire beyond our grasp, expressed in the dynamism of knowledge and love. But is that desire an absurd illusion, a deluding dream? Only God can be an adequate answer to mortal man's striving for the infinite. Up to this point, I have only expressed a philosophical statement. But even philosophically, is it rational not to consider the possibility that God might reveal himself to us, in order not to leave us in the miserable condition of a paradoxical and impossible desire?

Written for people who want to know—whether they are believers or not—what the Catholic Church claims to offer to humanity, this book will try to show the central role of the Church in human life. That will require several steps. In the first place, God reveals himself in his Son Jesus Christ. But how is it possible, two millennia after Christ's appearance and in the profusion of Christian and non-Christian religious systems, to know *that* and *how* this revelation could possibly reach us? If no sure answer can be given to this question, the good news of divine revelation will become a cynical joke that just adds to the delusion of our condition.

As God revealed himself, he secured a community where all would be invited not only to know him, but to share his life with him. Nothing less than that! This community was founded in order to last forever, in and beyond this world.

Thanks to the Church, divine revelation is preached and can be received with the certainty of faith. The typical Catholic certainty of having kept divine revelation in its purity is not pridefulness: It is humble gratitude to God who chooses to be faithful in spite of our sins. Without that Catholic certitude, expressed in the reality of "dogma," no Christian unity would be possible.

In the Church, God respects our nature. He respects his creature who is able to act in a free and rational way. He lets us cooperate in the diffusion of his revelation and even in the transmission of his divine grace. St. Thomas Aquinas's metaphysics show how divine action can use human actions. God acts in our actions.

Because our nature, which God respects, is to be both material (body) and spiritual (soul), the Church is always both visible and invisible. If that were not the case, God would not relate to us according to what we are. This is a fundamental insight of St. Thomas, applied to the Church by the Swiss cardinal Charles Journet, that clears away many "sociological" misunderstandings about what the Church is. The Body of Christ is not only a provider of nice social services. Aquinas sees all human beings as members—at least invited members—of the Church. Of course that helps solve some problems about how the Church relates to religious values in other denominations and in other religions. How can that be? Well: read.

In short, all desire God, whether consciously or not. And God can be found, because he has founded an everlasting community where we can share his life, and therefore where we find our joy. The good news of the incarnation of the Son of God is divine and human. We can receive that good news in a community where God acts in us and enlightens our re-created humanity.

CHAPTER ONE

Human Desire for God

THE HUMAN heart's desire for the infinite is so typical that to cancel it would mean to cancel humanity as such. This desire points toward God. Some pre-Christian philosophers noticed this characteristic feature of human nature, as well as a practical difficulty for its fulfillment.

The Dynamics of Human Acts according to Plato and Aristotle

It is impossible not to act. He who would stop doing anything whatsoever could not survive. Among human acts, two have a particular significance: knowledge and love. Ancient philosophers like Plato and Aristotle analyzed the meaning of human acts in a way that shows the relation of human acts to God, on the basis of some common dimensions of human life.

In his *Symposium*, Plato (ca. 427–347 B.C.) meditates upon love as a pursuit of beauty, according to a scale of more or less perfect beauty. The best thing would be to find a perfect and lasting beauty, but this is not easy:

> And the true order of going, or being led by another, to the things of love, is to begin from the beauties of earth and mount upwards

> for the sake of that other beauty, using these as steps only, and from one going on to two, and from two to all fair forms, and from fair forms to fair practices, and from fair practices to fair notions, until from fair notions he arrives at the notion of absolute beauty, and at last knows what the essence of beauty is. "This, my dear Socrates," said the stranger of Mantineia, "is that life above all others which man should live, in the contemplation of beauty absolute; a beauty which if you once beheld, you would see not to be after the measure of gold, and garments, and fair boys and youths, whose presence now entrances you; and you and many a one would be content to live seeing them only and conversing with them without meat or drink, if that were possible—you only want to look at them and to be with them. But what if man had eyes to see the true beauty—the divine beauty, I mean, pure and dear and unalloyed, not clogged with the pollutions of mortality and all the colours and vanities of human life—thither looking, and holding converse with the true beauty simple and divine? Remember how in that communion only, beholding beauty with the eye of the mind, he will be enabled to bring forth, not images of beauty, but realities (for he has hold not of an image but of a reality), and bringing forth and nourishing true virtue to become the friend of God and be immortal, if mortal man may. Would that be an ignoble life?"[1]

Thus, on the basis of one of the most common experiences of human life, Plato shows an infinite desire which would imply overcoming the basic limitation: death.

After Plato, Aristotle (ca. 384–322 B.C.) writes his *Nicomachean Ethics.* This moral treatise begins with a reflection on human acts that aim at some result. Like Plato's meditation on love, Aristotle deals with a basic dimension of human life: we act because we hope to get something from our actions. In order that different actions can be connected with each other, they must be organized in some hierarchy. For example, we work in order to earn some money in order to eat in order to live. If something is wished for

[1] Plato, *Symposium,* 211c–212a (trans. Benjamin Jowett).

its own sake and not for the sake of something else, then this might give some orientation to our whole life:

> Every art and every inquiry, and similarly every action and pursuit, is thought to aim at some good; and for this reason the good has rightly been declared to be that at which all things aim. . . . If, then, there is some end of the things we do, which we desire for its own sake (everything else being desired for the sake of this), and if we do not choose everything for the sake of something else (for at that rate the process would go on to infinity, so that our desire would be empty and vain), clearly this must be the good and the chief good. Will not the knowledge of it, then, have a great influence on life? Shall we not, like archers who have a mark to aim at, be more likely to hit upon what is right? If so, we must try, in outline at least, to determine what it is, and of which of the sciences or capacities it is the object. . . .[2]

After that general introduction to human acts, Aristotle suggests an identification of the supreme good with happiness:

> [I]f some activities are necessary, and desirable for the sake of something else, while others are so in themselves, evidently happiness must be placed among those desirable in themselves, not among those desirable for the sake of something else; for happiness does not lack anything, but is self-sufficient. Now those activities are desirable in themselves from which nothing is sought beyond the activity.[3]

He then identifies happiness with contemplation. "Contemplation" should not be identified with some specifically monastic or mystical activity (although it can also mean that, in another context). "Contemplation" simply means to see truth, which is the very purpose of our human intelligence, without which we would

---

[2] Aristotle, *Nicomachean Ethics,* I.i. 1–2, I.ii. 1–3 (trans. W. D. Ross).
[3] Ibid., X.vi. 2–3.

not be human. Aristotle is confronted, as Plato was, with the problem of death as a limitation to happiness:

> We think happiness has pleasure mingled with it, but the activity of philosophic wisdom is admittedly the pleasantest of virtuous activities; at all events the pursuit of it is thought to offer pleasures marvellous for their purity and their enduringness, and it is to be expected that those who know will pass their time more pleasantly than those who inquire. And the self-sufficiency that is spoken of must belong most to the contemplative activity. For while a philosopher, as well as a just man or one possessing any other virtue, needs the necessities of life, when they are sufficiently equipped with things of that sort the just man needs people towards whom and with whom he shall act justly, and the temperate man, the brave man, and each of the others is in the same case, but the philosopher, even when by himself, can contemplate truth, and the better the wiser he is; he can perhaps do so better if he has fellow-workers, but still he is the most self-sufficient. And this activity alone would seem to be loved for its own sake; for nothing arises from it apart from the contemplating, while from practical activities we gain more or less apart from the action. . . . So if among virtuous actions political and military actions are distinguished by nobility and greatness, and these are unleisurely and aim at an end and are not desirable for their own sake, but the activity of reason, which is contemplative, seems both to be superior in serious worth and to aim at no end beyond itself, and to have its pleasure proper to itself (and this augments the activity), and the self-sufficiency, leisureliness, unweariedness (so far as this is possible for man), and all the other attributes ascribed to the supremely happy man are evidently those connected with this activity, it follows that this will be the complete happiness of man, if it be allowed a complete term of life (for none of the attributes of happiness is incomplete). But such a life would be too high for man; for it is not insofar as he is man that he will live so, but insofar as something divine is present in him; and by so much as this is superior to our composite nature is its activity superior to that which is the exercise of the other kind of virtue. If reason is

> divine, then, in comparison with man, the life according to it is divine in comparison with human life. But we must not follow those who advise us, being men, to think of human things, and, being mortal, of mortal things, but must, so far as we can, make ourselves immortal, and strain every nerve to live in accordance with the best thing in us; for even if it be small in bulk, much more does it in power and worth surpass everything. This would seem, too, to be each man himself, since it is the authoritative and better part of him. It would be strange, then, if he were to choose not the life of his self but that of something else. And what we said before will apply now; that which is proper to each thing is by nature best and most pleasant for each thing; for man, therefore, the life according to reason is best and pleasantest, since reason more than anything else is man. This life therefore is also the happiest.[4]

The deep meaning of Aristotle's texts is that human actions require coordination. We need for our own life some architectonic principle: as it is impossible to build a house if all workers just keep moving without any global purpose, it is impossible to live a somehow efficient life without a main organizing principle. Aristotle identifies the underlying principle of all human actions with happiness. And human happiness is something that fits a rational animal: It implies the knowledge of truth.

Plato and Aristotle show that human life in its most basic and common characteristics—a search for love and knowledge—never really stops searching before it has reached an infinite satisfaction. Death is therefore a problem, highlighting the contrast between an infinite desire and finite capacities.

Thomas Aquinas (1224/25–1274)

St. Thomas Aquinas reads the ancient philosophers as a Christian: He sees the depth of their questions and of their answers, and adds some answers that come from his faith.

[4] Ibid., X.vii. 3–9.

Aquinas follows Aristotle quite strictly, saying that we need a final end to organize our actions:

> [I]f there were no last end, nothing would be desired, nor would any action have its term, nor would the intention of the agent be at rest; while if there is no first thing among those that are ordained to the end, none would begin to work at anything, and counsel would have no term, but would continue indefinitely.[5]

This final end is not *ad libitum*: Although we can choose among partial ends or means, we cannot not want to be happy (because we cannot not be human):

> As the intellect of necessity adheres to the first principles, the will must of necessity adhere to the last end, which is happiness.[6]

And the final end, without which the human heart cannot find peace, cannot be other than God. To show this, Thomas analyzes the dynamics of human knowledge, whose dynamics have also been made clear by the development of contemporary sciences:

> Final and perfect happiness can consist in nothing else than the vision of the Divine Essence. To make this clear, two points must be observed. First, that man is not perfectly happy, so long as something remains for him to desire and seek: secondly, that the perfection of any power is determined by the nature of its object. Now the object of the intellect is "what a thing is," i.e. the essence of a thing, according to *De Anima*. Wherefore the intellect attains perfection, in so far as it knows the essence of a thing. If therefore an intellect knows the essence of some effect, whereby it is not possible to know the essence of the cause, i.e. to know of the cause "what it is"; that intellect cannot be said to reach that cause simply, although it may be able to gather from the effect the knowledge

[5] Thomas Aquinas, *Summa theologiae (ST)* Ia IIae, q.1, a.4.
[6] *ST* Ia, q.82, a.1.

> that the cause is. Consequently, when man knows an effect, and knows that it has a cause, there naturally remains in the man the desire to know about the cause, "what it is." And this desire is one of wonder, and causes inquiry, as is stated in the beginning of the *Metaphysics*. For instance, if a man, knowing the eclipse of the sun, consider that it must be due to some cause, and know not what that cause is, he wonders about it, and from wondering proceeds to inquire. Nor does this inquiry cease until he arrive at a knowledge of the essence of the cause. If therefore the human intellect, knowing the essence of some created effect, knows no more of God than "that He is", the perfection of that intellect does not yet reach simply the First Cause, but there remains in it the natural desire to seek the cause. Wherefore it is not yet perfectly happy. Consequently, for perfect happiness the intellect needs to reach the very Essence of the First Cause. And thus it will have its perfection through union with God as with that object, in which alone man's happiness consists, as stated above.[7]

To know the final end matters supremely for all human actions. As long as we do not know it, we can make different kinds of mistakes, that is, substitute the final end with partial ends (a kind of idolatry), or choose the wrong means to reach the final end, or simply refuse God to be our final end. Only the vision of God can prevent such errors or refusals:

> There are certain individual goods which have not a necessary connection with happiness, because without them a man can be happy: and to such the will does not adhere of necessity. But there are some things which have a necessary connection with happiness, by means of which things man adheres to God, in Whom alone true happiness consists. Nevertheless, until through the certitude of the Divine Vision the necessity of such connection be shown, the will does not adhere to God of necessity, nor to those things which are of God. But the will of the man who sees God in

[7] *ST* Ia IIae, q.3, a.8.

> His essence of necessity adheres to God, just as now we desire of necessity to be happy.[8]

If such is our fulfillment, how do we obtain it?

SUMMARY

Human beings naturally act. This is not only a condition for surviving, but also the expression of human desires: we act because we want to get something, and all partial desires are somehow unified by the deep desire to be happy. Human happiness, given what we are, implies a fulfillment of both knowledge and love. The whole [of] human history (throughout different cultures), and also contemporary society, show that these desires are never fully satisfied. Whether we know it or not, even in our mistakes, we are striving for that happiness, which, since it is infinite, could be satisfied only by some infinite being, without the limitation of death. How is that going to happen?

From that point, there are two possibilities:

1. We try to satisfy ourselves with less than our fulfillment ;
2. God helps us. It would be irrational to exclude the possibility of some divine intervention, and I shall now try to show what this could mean.

---

[8] *ST* Ia, q.82, a.2.

CHAPTER TWO

Revelation

WHY WOULDN'T GOD LET US KNOW HIM?

OUR INFINITE DESIRE, as part of our nature, comes from God. If such a desire led only to frustration, God would have created human nature—his image—by mistake. Aquinas refutes such a possibility:

> If we should proceed to infinity in our desire for ends so that one end should always be desired on account of another to infinity, we will never arrive at the point where a man may attain the ends desired. But a man desires fruitlessly what he cannot get; consequently, the end he desires would be useless and vain. But this desire is natural, for it was said above that the good is what all beings naturally desire. Hence it follows that a natural desire would be useless and vain. But this is impossible. The reason is that a natural desire is nothing else but an inclination belonging to things by the disposition of the First Mover, and this cannot be frustrated.[1]

So that the human creature would not be absurd, God has given us a way to him:

[1] Thomas Aquinas, *Sententia Libri Ethicorum,* Book 1, lectio 2, §3.

> It is the nature of the human mind to gather its knowledge from sensible things; nor can it of itself arrive at the direct vision of the divine substance, as that substance is in itself raised above all sensible things and all other beings to boot, and beyond all proportion with them. But because the perfect good of man consists in his knowing God in such way as he can, there is given man a way of ascending to the knowledge of God, to the end that so noble a creature should not seem to exist altogether in vain, unable to attain the proper end of his existence.[2]

For Aquinas, God reveals himself "ex superabundanti bonitate"[3] (because of his superabundant goodness). The Second Vatican Council says that "In His goodness and wisdom God chose to reveal Himself."[4] To say that God reveals himself out of goodness underlines both the help we receive and the divine freedom. Pope Pius XII goes further. He first insists on the difficulty of our knowledge of God, both because God is infinitely higher than ourselves, but also because we are afraid of conversion:

> Though human reason is, strictly speaking, truly capable by its own natural power and light of attaining to a true and certain knowledge of the one personal God who watches over and governs the world by his providence, and of the natural law written in our hearts by the Creator; yet there are many obstacles which prevent reason from the effective and fruitful use of this inborn faculty. For the truths that refer to God and concern the relations between God and our human race wholly transcend the visible order of things, and, if they are translated into human action and influence it, they call for self-surrender and abnegation. The human mind, in its turn, is hampered in the attaining of such truths, not only by the impact of the senses and the imagination,

---

[2] Thomas Aquinas, *Summa contra Gentiles,* Book IV, chap. 1.

[3] Ibid.

[4] Vatican Council II, Dogmatic Constitution on Divine Revelation, *Dei Verbum* (18 November 1965), §1.

> but also by disordered appetites which are the consequences of original sin. So it happens that people in such matters easily persuade themselves that what they would not like to be true is false or at least doubtful.[5]

Given this situation, the pope says that revelation is even morally necessary:

> Hence we have to admit that divine revelation is morally necessary in order that such religious and moral truths "which of themselves are not beyond human reason can, even in the present condition of humankind, be known by everyone with facility, with firm certitude and with no admixture of error."[6]

To speak about a moral necessity on the side of God is very strong, and "moral" should not be forgotten: God is not strictly obliged to help us. Such a "necessity" depends on previous free divine actions, above all on the creation of a creature who is in the divine image and cannot be fully itself without God.

Even if one admits at least a probability of divine revelation, what does that say about the Church? Does revelation imply a structured community like the Church? Does it imply one community?

Purpose of Revelation: God Wants to Share His Communion

In order to understand the means used for divine revelation and for its transmission, one must see what the purpose of revelation is. If that purpose were only to give us some information about God, it might be sufficient to give bits of information to several groups, who would have to put it together—along with many

[5] Pius XII, Encyclical *Humani Generis*, 12 August 1950; Denzinger 3875; *The Christian Faith*, 6th ed., Jacques Dupuis (New York: Alba House, 1996), §144.

[6] Encyclical *Humani Generis*; Denzinger, 3876; *The Christian Faith*, 145.

ideas—in order to have a complete picture. But the purpose of revelation is far higher than that.

Three texts that express the most characteristic features of Christian faith highlight divine Revelation in Jesus Christ as infinitely higher than any other knowledge of God, and the fact that this revelation achieves infinitely more than a merely good human life:

> In the beginning was the Word, and the Word was with God, and the Word was God. He was with God in the beginning. Through him all things were made; without him nothing was made that has been made. In him was life, and that life was the light of men. The light shines in the darkness, but the darkness has not understood it. . . . He came to that which was his own, but his own did not receive him. Yet to all who received him, to those who believed in his name, he gave the right to become children of God—children born not of natural descent, nor of human decision or a husband's will, but born of God.[7]
>
> But when the time had fully come, God sent his Son, born of a woman, born under the law, to redeem those under the law, that we might receive the full rights of sons. Because you are sons, God sent the Spirit of his Son into our hearts, the Spirit who calls out, "Abba, Father." So you are no longer a slave, but a son; and since you are a son, God has made you also an heir.[8]
>
> Simon Peter, a servant and apostle of Jesus Christ, to those who through the righteousness of our God and Savior Jesus Christ have received a faith as precious as ours: Grace and peace be yours in abundance through the knowledge of God and of Jesus our Lord. His divine power has given us everything we need for life and godliness through our knowledge of him who called us by his own glory and goodness. Through these he has given us his very great and precious promises, so that through them you may participate in the divine nature and escape the corruption in the world caused by evil desires.[9]

---

[7] John 1:1–4, 11–13.
[8] Galatians 4:4–7.
[9] Peter 1:1–4.

These texts, which the Church offers as readings during Christmas time,[10] all say that the effect of the Incarnation of the Son of God—in other words of divine revelation—is to offer us the possibility to share divine life. We can become children of God, and children have the same type of life as their parents. Vatican II's Dogmatic Constitution on Divine Revelation summarizes that biblical teaching:

> In His goodness and wisdom God chose to reveal Himself and to make known to us the hidden purpose of His will by which, through Christ, the Word made flesh, man might in the Holy Spirit have access to the Father and come to share in the divine nature.[11]

One might be surprised to hear that the baptized receive divine life, since the life of Christians seems to be quite human, especially since it is still affected by sin and suffering, and some even challenge the Christian claim precisely because of that.[12] The way we receive our participation in divine life in this world is already real, but still hidden. We are not yet in the beatific vision, that is, the fully happy vision of God:

> How great is the love the Father has lavished on us, that we should be called children of God! And that is what we are! The reason the world does not know us is that it did not know him. Dear friends, now we are children of God, and what we will be has not yet been

---

[10] At Roman Rite Masses.

[11] Vatican Council II, Dogmatic Constitution on Divine Revelation, *Dei Verbum,* §2.

[12] Cf. John Hick, *The Rainbow of Faiths, Critical Dialogues on Religious Pluralism* (London: SCM, 1995), 15–16: "Our traditional theology tells us that Jesus of Nazareth was God. . . . If our traditional Christian theology is true, surely we should expect these fruits to be present more fully in Christians generally than in non-Christians generally. . . . But I have been suggesting that, so far as we can tell, these visible fruits do not occur more abundantly among Christians than among Jews, Muslims, Hindus, Buddhists, Sikhs, Taoists, Baha'is, and so on."

> made known. But we know that when he appears, we shall be like him, for we shall see him as he is. Everyone who has this hope in him purifies himself, just as he is pure.[13]

Our task as children of God in this world is to thank him for his love and to prepare ourselves for the Vision. This is summarized in love, as a response to divine love and participation in it:

> We know that we have passed from death to life, because we love our brothers. Anyone who does not love remains in death. Anyone who hates his brother is a murderer, and you know that no murderer has eternal life in him. This is how we know what love is: Jesus Christ laid down his life for us. And we ought to lay down our lives for our brothers. If anyone has material possessions and sees his brother in need but has no pity on him, how can the love of God be in him? Dear children, let us not love with words or tongue but with actions and in truth. This then is how we know that we belong to the truth, and how we set our hearts at rest in his presence whenever our hearts condemn us. For God is greater than our hearts, and he knows everything.[14]

If the purpose of revelation is to make us share divine life, it must obviously come from God himself, and it seems that it must come from God alone, for a reason explained by Aquinas:

> The gift of grace surpasses every capability of created nature, since it is nothing short of a partaking of the Divine Nature, which exceeds every other nature. And thus it is impossible that any creature should cause grace. For it is as necessary that God alone should deify, bestowing a partaking of the Divine Nature by a participated likeness.[15]

Of course divine revelation, by definition, comes from God. Only God can pull us up to his own life. We see here that Revela-

[13] 1 John 3:1–3.
[14] 1 John 3:14–20.
[15] *ST* Ia IIae, q.112, a.1.

tion and Salvation are just two different ways of looking at the same divine action. God acts in this world to help us know him, even offering human beings a vision that is a participation in his life. Whoever then fully accepts divine revelation, with the necessary help of grace, takes part in salvation. Our salvation is "Christ, who is both the mediator and the fullness of all revelation."[16]

It seems that Christ saves individuals only by his own immediate action. Two questions arise then: Could divine action bring about the Church, and could the Church take any part in divine saving action? I begin with the first point: the Church is man's communion with God, which communion is the purpose of divine revelation.

The Communion Achieved by Revelation/Salvation is the Church

Human communities usually arise out of common needs, common interests, shared passions. Human families especially are constituted by some shared life. Human beings who receive divine life are, because of this gift, a community with God and among themselves. And the consciousness of the gift received lets them invite others to share that gift. This is what Vatican II says, quoting the first letter of St. John:

> Hearing the word of God with reverence and proclaiming it with faith, the sacred synod takes its direction from these words of St. John: "We announce to you the eternal life which dwelt with the Father and was made visible to us. What we have seen and heard we announce to you, so that you may have fellowship with us and our common fellowship is with the Father and His Son Jesus Christ" (1 John 1:2–3).[17]

---

16 *Dei Verbum,* §2.

17 Ibid., §1. cf. §2: "Through this revelation, therefore, the invisible God out of the abundance of His love speaks to men as friends and lives among them, so that He may invite and take them into fellowship with Himself."

A communion with God results from divine action in the world. Developments in the theology of the Church in recent decades—both in Catholic theology and in the ecumenical movement—let the Church be described precisely as a "communion." John Paul II identified this relatively new way of speaking about the Church as a key to all Vatican II's documents.[18] If the notion of communion describes the relations within the Church (the whole People of God and the clergy, all bishops with the bishop of Rome, Christians of different denominations in perfect or only partial communion), it expresses in the very first place the relation to God. Divine action among human beings creates a communion, and this communion is the Church. The communion of the Church is the result and the purpose of revelation. If this sounds too outrageously Catholic, it might be useful to notice what John Calvin, one of the fathers of the Protestant Reformation, wrote in his *Geneva Catechism*:

- What is the Church?
- The body and society of believers whom God hath predestined to eternal life.
- Is it necessary to believe this article also?
- Yes, verily, if we would not make the death of Christ without effect, and set at nought all that has hitherto been said. For the one effect [in the French text: *le fruit,* the fruit] resulting from all is that there is a Church.[19]

Even though this text presupposes a particular conception of predestination that the Catholic Church has never shared and that

[18] Cf. John Paul II, Encyclical *Ecclesia de Eucharistia* (17 April 2003), §34: "The Extraordinary Assembly of the Synod of Bishops in 1985 saw in the concept of an 'ecclesiology of communion' the central and fundamental idea of the documents of the Second Vatican Council."

[19] John Calvin, *Catechism,* section 15.

many contemporary Protestants do not share either (but this is not our present topic), it clearly says that the Church is the fruit of divine action in Christ. This is well expressed in terms of communion: divine communion resulting in a human communion, or in a divine-human communion. Similar insights are expressed in the biblical term of Body of Christ.

Christ and His Body

St. Paul speaks of the Church as the Body of Christ, in which the different members are united by the Holy Spirit:

> The body is a unit, though it is made up of many parts; and though all its parts are many, they form one body. So it is with Christ. For we were all baptized by one Spirit into one body—whether Jews or Greeks, slave or free—and we were all given the one Spirit to drink. Now the body is not made up of one part but of many. . . . If one part suffers, every part suffers with it; if one part is honored, every part rejoices with it. Now you are the body of Christ, and each one of you is a part of it. And in the church God has appointed first of all apostles, second prophets, third teachers, then workers of miracles, also those having gifts of healing, those able to help others, those with gifts of administration, and those speaking in different kinds of tongues.[20]

Because of the unity between Christ—the Head—and his Body, the Lord can ask Saul right before his conversion: "Saul, Saul, why do you persecute me,"[21] and not: "Why do you persecute them?"

Vatican II explains that the Body is constituted as a new creation, a new life, built in this world by the Holy Spirit diffusing salvation, that is, the life of the risen Lord Jesus Christ, in the sacraments:

> In the human nature united to Himself the Son of God, by overcoming death through His own death and resurrection, redeemed

[20] 1 Corinthians 12:12–28.

[21] Acts 9:4.

man and re-molded him into a new creation. By communicating His Spirit, Christ made His brothers, called together from all nations, mystically the components of His own Body. In that Body the life of Christ is poured into the believers who, through the sacraments, are united in a hidden and real way to Christ who suffered and was glorified. Through Baptism we are formed in the likeness of Christ: "For in one Spirit we were all baptized into one body." In this sacred rite a oneness with Christ's death and resurrection is both symbolized and brought about: "For we were buried with Him by means of Baptism into death"; and if "we have been united with Him in the likeness of His death, we shall be so in the likeness of His resurrection also." Really partaking of the body of the Lord in the breaking of the eucharistic bread, we are taken up into communion with Him and with one another. "Because the bread is one, we though many, are one body, all of us who partake of the one bread." In this way all of us are made members of His Body, "but severally members one of another."[22]

As the Church is the communion, which is the purpose of the redeeming revelation, she is also the Body constituted by the life of the risen Christ. The resurrection of Christ was not for himself (for that he did not need to take a human nature), but for the Church:

Christ's soul is moved by God through grace, not only so as to reach the glory of life everlasting, but so as to lead others to it, inasmuch as He is the Head of the Church, and the Author of human salvation.[23]

Where eternal life—our salvation—is, the Church is. This is why St. Thomas Aquinas could say that, one way or another, all human beings belong to the Church:

We must say that if we take the whole time of the world in general, Christ is the Head of all human beings, but diversely. For, first and

[22] Council Vatican II, Dogmatic Constitution on the Church, *Lumen Gentium* (21 November 1964), §7.

[23] *ST* Ia IIae, q. 114, a. 6.

> principally, He is the Head of such as are united to Him by glory; secondly, of those who are actually united to Him by charity; thirdly, of those who are actually united to Him by faith; fourthly, of those who are united to Him merely in potentiality, which is not yet reduced to act, yet will be reduced to act according to Divine predestination; fifthly, of those who are united to Him in potentiality, which will never be reduced to act; such are those men existing in the world, who are not predestined, who, however, on their departure from this world, wholly cease to be members of Christ, as being no longer in potentiality to be united to Christ.[24]

For Aquinas, then, to be a member of the Church means to be united to Christ, in other words, to receive salvation by divine grace. Christ is "the head of all human beings in regard to grace."[25] I will develop later on what this means for non-Catholics and for non-Christians. The point here is only to show the link between salvation and the Church: the edification of the Body of Christ is the immediate purpose of the whole work of Christ. Christ acting in the Holy Spirit builds a community that in a way becomes himself. As St. Paul says rather paradoxically, the risen Lord has been made "the ruler of everything, the head of the Church, which is the body, the fullness of him who fills the whole creation."[26] Because the Son of God did not come into our world for himself—he would not have needed it—but for us, his work is only achieved in the constitution of his Body. This is why St. Augustine can say "totus christus, caput, et corpus"[27] (the whole Christ, head and body).

SUMMARY

Without God, our human desires of knowledge and love cannot be fulfilled, up to the point that humanity as such would be simply

---

[24] *ST* IIIa, q.8, a.3.
[25] *ST* IIIa, q.19, a.4, ad 1.
[26] Ephesians 1:22–23.
[27] Augustine, *Enarratio in Psalmum* 74, 4: CCSL 39, 1027.

absurd. For St. Thomas Aquinas, an absurd creature would be some kind of divine mistake, and he denies that God would do this. In any case, it is at least reasonable to consider the possibility that God would let himself be known to us.

Christians believe that God revealed himself, not only in order to give us some information about him, but to call us to share his own life, without end—to be in communion with him. And this communion is precisely the communion of the Church, which begins in this world and goes on fully in the next life.

God reveals himself in his incarnate Son Jesus Christ. The Son of God did not come into our world for himself: the fulfillment of the work of the incarnation is in the Body of Christ, namely the Church.

CHAPTER THREE

The Church Lasts as Long as Christ's Work

THE DIVINE PURPOSE in revelation/salvation is far-reaching. The existence of the Church is strictly linked to that divine purpose. We shall now see why the Church is going to last forever, although some of her features will pass.

THE PURPOSE OF REVELATION—SALVATION IS NOT LIMITED IN TIME

The purpose of Christ's action is not limited to a particular human group in a particular part of the world or during a particular period. God wants to gather humanity into communion with himself, and the Church is the instrument chosen for that work, or more precisely for the diffusion of the work of Christ:

> Christ is the Light of nations. Because this is so, this Sacred Synod gathered together in the Holy Spirit eagerly desires, by proclaiming the Gospel to every creature, to bring the light of Christ to all men, a light brightly visible on the countenance of the Church. Since the Church is in Christ like a sacrament or as a sign and instrument both of a very closely knit union with God and of the unity of the whole human race, it desires now to unfold more

> fully to the faithful of the Church and to the whole world its own inner nature and universal mission.[1]

God would not have revealed himself if it would have been for a short time only. He knows how fast we would forget, break, or modify his gifts. Therefore, as Vatican II says, the very reason for which God revealed himself is also the reason why he provided some means for the transmission of that revelation:

> In His gracious goodness, God has seen to it that what He had revealed for the salvation of all nations would abide perpetually in its full integrity and be handed on to all generations.[2]

That work of transmission was therefore accomplished. The choice by Christ of twelve apostles among the disciples was a first step in that direction: they received specific gifts to support the other disciples in their faith. When important questions arose, the apostles gave answers to the whole community. It is striking to see how they could decide that Christians would not have to be circumcised, nor would they have to observe many precepts of the law of Moses[3] (about food, for instance), although Christians as well as Jews believed and still believe that all these precepts had been given to his chosen people by God himself. How could the apostles have done that if not on the basis of some authority given to them by the same one who had given the Law to Moses, that is, God himself?

> You have heard that it was said to the people long ago, "Do not murder, and anyone who murders will be subject to judgment." But I tell you that anyone who is angry with his brother will be subject to judgment. Again, anyone who says to his brother, "Raca," is answerable to the Sanhedrin. But anyone who says,

[1] *Lumen Gentium,* §1.
[2] *Dei Verbum,* §7.
[3] Cf. Acts 15.

> "You fool!" will be in danger of the fire of hell.[4] [T]he Son of Man is Lord of the Sabbath.[5]

The freedom Jesus had had in relation to the Law is thus given to the apostles. But what happens when the apostles themselves die? Once again, for the same reason that divine revelation has been given in the first place and that it has been secured thanks to the apostolic ministry, the apostles appoint successors. Vatican II summarizes these steps:

> Christ the Lord in whom the full revelation of the supreme God is brought to completion, commissioned the Apostles to preach to all men that Gospel which is the source of all saving truth and moral teaching, and to impart to them heavenly gifts. This Gospel had been promised in former times through the prophets, and Christ Himself had fulfilled it and promulgated it with His lips. This commission was faithfully fulfilled by the Apostles who, by their oral preaching, by example, and by observances [Latin: *institutiones*[6]/institutions] handed on what they had received from the lips of Christ, from living with Him, and from what He did, or what they had learned through the prompting of the Holy Spirit. The commission was fulfilled, too, by those Apostles and apostolic men who under the inspiration of the same Holy Spirit committed the message of salvation to writing.[7]

Of course that text does not address the historical complexity of apostolic succession, namely how the Church passed from the apostolic time itself to a situation in which every local church would have one bishop, perceived as distinct from the priests. I shall address the relation between historical knowledge and theology in Chapter Four. For now, about our precise point, I simply follow Hermann Pottmeyer:

[4] Matthew 5:21–22.

[5] Matthew 12:8.

[6] In the text the word is declined: *institutionibus*.

[7] *Dei Verbum*, §7.

> The causes which have led to the development and the establishment of the hierarchical episcopacy are assessed in various ways by historical research. There is agreement on the fact that a group of causes was in play. Whereas historians see the complex conditioning of development, faith recognizes in the historical unfolding the result of the conduct of events by God.[8]

Certainly the process leading to a unified way of organizing the local churches needed some time—as the recognition of the content of the Bible also needed some time—but Vatican II summarizes that process by reading it with the eyes of faith in divine action through history.

Dei Verbum 7 mentions the elements of the apostolic testimony:

1. Preaching
2. Example
3. Institutions
4. Writing the New Testament

I will now comment on what these four elements suggest about the continuity of the Church after the death of the apostles. I will introduce this with some precision about what it means for the bishops to be the apostles' successors.

The Apostles and Their Successors

How can the apostles have successors? Part of their specific ministry depends on their being witnesses of the life, death, and resurrection of Christ. This is why, when the apostles want to choose a successor for Judas, they express the following criterion:

---

[8] Hermann J. Pottmeyer, "Bischof," *Lexikon für Theologie und Kirche,* Bd.2, (Freiburg im Br.: Herder, 1994), 3rd. ed., col. 484–85. (My translation.)

> Therefore it is necessary to choose one of the men who have been with us the whole time the Lord Jesus went in and out among us, beginning from John's baptism to the time when Jesus was taken up from us. For one of these must become a witness with us of his resurrection.[9]

The visions St. Paul had of Jesus substitute for that kind of direct experience, and still make him a specific kind of apostle.

Is it then possible to envisage successors of the apostles? In an argument quite central for the Reformation, Calvin insisted on a basic difference between the apostles and their successors (whoever they might be):

> Although, as I have observed, there is this difference between the apostles and their successors, they were sure and authentic amanuenses of the Holy Spirit; and, therefore, their writings are to be regarded as the oracles of God, whereas others have no other office than to teach what is delivered and sealed in the holy Scriptures. We conclude, therefore, that it does not now belong to faithful ministers to coin some new doctrine, but simply to adhere to the doctrine to which all, without exceptions, are made subject. When I say this, I mean to show not only what each individual, but what the whole Church, is bound to do. In regard to individuals, Paul certainly had been appointed an apostle to the Corinthians, and yet he declares that he has no dominion over their faith (2 Cor 1: 24). Who will now presume to arrogate a dominion to which the apostle declares that he himself was not competent? Then the reason to which we ought here to have regard is universal: God deprives man of the power of producing any new doctrine, in order that he alone may be our master in spiritual teaching, as he alone is true, and can neither lie nor deceive. This reason applies not less to the whole Church than to every individual believer.[10]

---

[9] Acts 1:21–22.

[10] John Calvin, *Institutes of Christian Religion,* IV.8.9.

There is certainly a point to what Calvin has said: Catholics do not have to claim that bishops are in all ways successors of the apostles. The episcopal ministry is a permanent necessity in the Church but does not include all elements of the ministry of the apostles themselves. In the first place, it does not include the necessity of having been eyewitnesses of the life of Jesus two millennia ago. The reason the apostles have successors is that some part of their ministry will always be necessary:

> That divine mission, entrusted by Christ to the apostles, will last until the end of the world, since the Gospel they are to teach is for all time the source of all life for the Church. And for this reason the apostles, appointed as rulers in this society, took care to appoint successors.[11]

After this initial precision, I move to the four elements of the apostolic testimony mentioned in *Dei Verbum* 7.

PREACHING

Jesus preached. The apostles and their successors also preach because he has sent them to do so, promising to help them in that task:

> Therefore go and make disciples of all nations, baptizing them in the name of the Father and of the Son and of the Holy Spirit, and teaching them to obey everything I have commanded you. And surely I am with you always, to the very end of the age.[12]

The preaching implies sharing in both Jesus' dangerous mission and, somehow, in Jesus' authority:

> Go! I am sending you out like lambs among wolves. Do not take a purse or bag or sandals; and do not greet anyone on the road. . . .

---

[11] *Lumen Gentium,* §20.
[12] Matthew 28:19–20.

> He who listens to you listens to me; he who rejects you rejects me; but he who rejects me rejects him who sent me.[13]

This preaching by the disciples is the way Jesus chooses to let his Good News be known. Because of this conditional necessity, St. Paul then says:

> How, then, can they call on the one they have not believed in? And how can they believe in the one of whom they have not heard? And how can they hear without someone preaching to them? And how can they preach unless they are sent?[14]

In the next chapter I shall try to show some implications of this preaching, above all how people who live 2,000 years after Christ can know whether what they are told is in continuity with Christ's teaching. For now, we already see that the apostles have been sent to preach so that others could believe. And this necessity of having people proclaim their faith so that others believe is no less urgent in the third millennium than it was in the first century. In that regard, the apostles need some successors.

Example of Life

The apostles, like Jesus before them, announced him also by the example of their life. This is a constant tenet of divine revelation, as *Dei Verbum* pointed out:

> This plan of revelation is realized by deeds and words having an inner unity: the deeds wrought by God in the history of salvation manifest and confirm the teaching and realities signified by the words, while the words proclaim the deeds and clarify the mystery contained in them.[15]

---

[13] Luke 10:3–4, 16.
[14] Romans 10:14–15.
[15] *Dei Verbum,* §2.

Already in the Old Testament, word and action go together (the Hebrew word *dabar* can mean both). God speaks to Abraham or to Moses, but they also know him thanks to his actions: he gives the Promised Land, and frees his people several times. In the New Testament the history of Jesus is certainly as important as his words: he not only speaks, he lives with us and gives his life. The whole sacramental life of the Church expresses the same: in the sacraments neither words alone ("I baptize you," without water) nor acts alone (pouring water on somebody without any word) are sufficient. The example of the saints in the life of the Church supports the preaching, and their life is understandable thanks to the preaching of the Gospel. As Cardinal Ratzinger underlined in a symposium about John Paul II held at the Angelicum University in Rome, the pope added many canonizations to his doctrinal teaching precisely because of his conviction that both words and deeds show Christian life.[16]

Of course the visible examples of how God can transform a human life are as necessary nowadays as they were at the time of the apostles. It is also clear that these examples are not to be seen only in bishops: as all disciples of Christ were called to show their dignity in their life, all present disciples are called to holiness. As Aquinas said, "The distinction of states and duties is not an obstacle to the unity of the Church, for this results from the unity of faith, charity, and mutual service."[17] Vatican II shows how laypeople give a specific example of the Christian life that is common to all members of the Church:

> These faithful are by baptism made one body with Christ and are constituted among the People of God; they are in their own way

[16] Cf. Joseph Ratzinger, "'Teologia sapienzale'. Sollecitudine di Giovanni Paolo II per il terzo millenio," *Fede di studioso e obbedienza di pastore,* Atti del Convegno sul 50° del Dottorato di K. Wojtyla e del 20° del Pontificato di Giovanni Paolo II, a cura di Edward Kaczynski (Roma: Millennium Romae, 1999), 82.

[17] *ST* IIa IIae, q.183, a.2, a.1.

> made sharers in the priestly, prophetical, and kingly functions of Christ; and they carry out for their own part the mission of the whole Christian people in the Church and in the world. What specifically characterizes the laity is their secular nature. It is true that those in holy orders can at times be engaged in secular activities, and even have a secular profession. But they are by reason of their particular vocation especially and professedly ordained to the sacred ministry. Similarly, by their state in life, religious give splendid and striking testimony that the world cannot be transformed and offered to God without the spirit of the beatitudes. But the laity, by their very vocation, seek the kingdom of God by engaging in temporal affairs and by ordering them according to the plan of God. They live in the world, that is, in each and in all of the secular professions and occupations. They live in the ordinary circumstances of family and social life, from which the very web of their existence is woven. They are called there by God that by exercising their proper function and led by the spirit of the Gospel they may work for the sanctification of the world from within as a leaven. In this way they may make Christ known to others, especially by the testimony of a life resplendent in faith, hope and charity.[18]

As I previously said about preaching, examples of Christian life are necessary so that the world may be able to receive divine revelation, that is, to be in communion with God. The apostles and their successors chose that double and inseparable way of communication, and such a necessity has not disappeared ever since. In other words, the necessity of the Church, preaching and living the Gospel, remains nowadays because of the very purpose of divine revelation itself.

Institutions in a People

Dei Verbum 7 says that the apostles handed on what they have received also by establishing institutions *(institutiones)*. As the

---

[18] *Lumen Gentium,* §31.

Protestant theologian Everett Ferguson says, institutions are part of the impact of divine action in the world:

> Properly understood, "to be in the church is to be in Christ, and to be in Christ is to be in the church." One is not "in Christ" because of being "in the church," but one is "in the church" because of being "in Christ." Membership in the church is not a matter of separate choice by the one joined to Christ (as if one could belong to Christ and not belong to his people). To be saved is to be a Christian, and to be a Christian is to be a member of the church. God by the same action that saves places the person in the redeemed community. Nor is the church in the Bible an invisible body. . . . The church is part of God's redemptive plan. . . . Paul as a missionary did not simply make converts; he planted and built churches.[19]

That text is quite complete and shows that Christian preaching is not directed only to individual salvation or knowledge but to the building up of a community. In the Catholic and Orthodox perspective, it is obvious that Baptism and catechesis must lead to the Eucharist, which implies a local Church gathered around a bishop. To proclaim the Word of God includes such institutional dimensions because human beings are naturally social animals and keep their nature even as they are redeemed. The institutional character of the Church is intrinsically linked to the social character of human life. If God cares about individuals, then his purpose is not to deal with them only individually:

> At all times and in every race God has given welcome to whosoever fears Him and does what is right. God, however, does not make men holy and save them merely as individuals, without bond or link between one another. Rather has it pleased Him to bring men together as one people, a people which acknowledges Him in truth and serves Him in holiness.[20]

[19] Everett Ferguson, *The Church of Christ: A Biblical Ecclesiology for Today* (Grand Rapids, MI: W. B. Eerdmans, 1996), 205.

[20] *Lumen Gentium,* §9.

Why the Christian community should be structured will be dealt with in the next chapters. For now I just mention that to preach the Gospel implies to build a community with certain key features, as the Acts of the Apostles shows in explaining the fact and the consequences of some conversions:

> With many other words he [Peter] warned them; and he pleaded with them, "Save yourselves from this corrupt generation." Those who accepted his message were baptized, and about three thousand were added to their number that day. They devoted themselves to the apostles' teaching and to the fellowship, to the breaking of bread and to prayer.[21]

Nowadays also a conversion to the Lord Jesus Christ implies fidelity to the teaching of the apostles and to the breaking of bread thanks to which the disciples of Emmaus had recognized Jesus.[22] Such consequences implied and still imply an organized community.

WRITING THE NEW TESTAMENT

In its description of the apostolic teaching, *Dei Verbum* 7 mentions a last element: "The commission was fulfilled, too, by those Apostles and apostolic men who under the inspiration of the same Holy Spirit committed the message of salvation to writing." This passage is about the writing of the New Testament. I shall comment later about the relationship between divine inspiration and human authors. For now I stress the fact that first, Christ had not written any text himself (he had perhaps written on the ground[23] and he might have written something else, but he left no text); second, the apostles had been preaching and planting the Church for years before they—with others—wrote the texts of the New Testament;

[21] Acts 2:40–42.
[22] Cf. Luke 24:30–31.
[23] Cf. John 8:6.

and finally, the precise determination of the content of the Bible took centuries.

Aquinas sees several reasons why Jesus did not write himself:

> It was fitting that Christ should not commit His doctrine to writing. First, on account of His dignity: for the more excellent the teacher, the more excellent should be his manner of teaching. Consequently it was fitting that Christ, as the most excellent of teachers, should adopt that manner of teaching whereby His doctrine is imprinted on the hearts of His hearers. . . . And so it was that among the Gentiles, Pythagoras and Socrates, who were teachers of great excellence, were unwilling to write anything. For writings are ordained, as to an end, unto the imprinting of doctrine in the hearts of the hearers. Secondly, on account of the excellence of Christ's doctrine, which cannot be expressed in writing; according to Jn. 21:25: "There are also many other things which Jesus did: which, if they were written everyone, the world itself, I think, would not be able to contain the books that should be written." Which Augustine explains by saying: "We are not to believe that in respect of space the world could not contain them . . . but that by the capacity of the readers they could not be comprehended." And if Christ had committed His doctrine to writing, men would have had no deeper thought of His doctrine than that which appears on the surface of the writing. Thirdly, that His doctrine might reach all in an orderly manner: Himself teaching His disciples immediately, and they subsequently teaching others, by preaching and writing: whereas if He Himself had written, His doctrine would have reached all immediately.[24]

This text reminds us first that the purpose of revelation is to change human hearts so that our life becomes divine life. It then recalls that such a purpose is infinite and cannot be limited by paper and letters. Finally it describes what actually happened in history: Christ teaches his disciples of later times through disci-

[24] *ST* IIIa, q.42, a.4.

ples of previous times. This is the order of transmission of revelation that appears first in the New Testament itself.

Of course at a certain point the apostles and some others wrote the texts of our contemporary New Testament. This is of first importance, and once the New Testament, inspired by the Holy Spirit, had been written, it received a unique authority. This is why the New Testament's relation to the Church must be well understood.

Three main questions appear:

1. Who is the author of the Bible?
2. How do we know what the Bible is?
3. What is the authority of biblical texts, compared to other texts, and of different interpretations of the Bible?

I shall deal now with the first two questions, leaving the third one for my next chapter.

Who is the Author of the Bible?

The authorship of the Bible is a point of primary importance. Are the alternatives simply that either God is its author or it has been written by human beings? Such a question creates huge difficulties for Muslims to whom the Koran is simply the word of God himself. Every part of it is said by God, in Arabic, and therefore any discrepancy between this book and, for example, contemporary science obliges us to choose between the two. Some believers will then feel obliged to reject contemporary science as a lie of the western world. The implicit "scientific" worldview of both the Bible and the Koran was more or less identical to academic "scientific" views at least until the sixteenth century, but since then the difference has increased at an accelerating rate. Such an evolution has obliged believers to deepen their understanding of the status of revealed texts, highlighting the difference between a divine level

and a human level. Some Christian fundamentalists understand revelation as Muslims do: no real human part, only a direct divine act. Most contemporary Christian theologians, however, recognize the role of human authors. But on the other hand, if the Bible is simply a human book (an extreme consequence of some liberal views), there is no revelation any more, and the influence of the Bible wanes (for instance, biblical moral teaching can simply be reversed, as the expression of a past culture). There is no reason why Catholics should have to accept either of these views.

Vatican II says that both God (i.e., the Holy Spirit inspiring) and certain men are the authors of the Bible:

> Holy mother Church, relying on the belief of the Apostles (see John 20:31; 2 Tim 3:16; 2 Peter 1:19–20, 3:15–6), holds that the books of both the Old and New Testaments in their entirety, with all their parts, are sacred and canonical because, written under the inspiration of the Holy Spirit, they have God as their author and have been handed on as such to the Church herself. In composing the sacred books, God chose men, and while employed by Him, they made use of their powers and abilities, so that with Him acting in them and through them, they, as true authors, consigned to writing everything and only those things which He wanted.[25]

Does that mean that God wrote part of the Bible, the most important or most beautiful texts, and men other parts? Certainly not. All texts were written by men—the apostles and others with them—under divine inspiration. The human authors are true authors, with their culture, their language, their style (beautiful or not) and so on. What they express necessarily implies a worldview of their time: they were not supposed to know Galileo and Einstein, and this was not necessary for the communication of the basic truth of faith that God created the world. Divine inspiration means that what these human authors wrote with their words and within a pro-

[25] *Dei Verbum,* §11.

gression (Christians thus read the Old Testament in the light of Jesus Christ) would be what could show us the way to salvation:

> Since everything asserted by the inspired authors or sacred writers must be held to be asserted by the Holy Spirit, it follows that the books of Scripture must be acknowledged as teaching solidly, faithfully and without error that truth which God wanted put into sacred writings for the sake of salvation.[26]

The first president of the Vatican's Dicastery of Ecumenism (first called Secretariat for Christian Unity), the German cardinal Augustine Bea, who was also a biblical scholar, attributed to St. Thomas Aquinas the keys that allowed Christians to see the kind of collaboration between God and human biblical authors:

> The second category of considerations forming a starting-point for this doctrine of inspiration concerns God's manner of influencing the prophets. Here we turn to the Old Testament for guidance, and are indebted to St. Thomas Aquinas for his assertion, after mature reflection, that the authors of the sacred books are God's instruments indeed, but living instruments who, even when being used by God, do not cease to be their complete selves and therefore act as intelligent and free agents, neither more nor less than would any other human authors. This concept of "instrumentality" as an explanation for the mode of inspiration of the sacred books was expounded by Pius XII in *Divino afflante Spiritu*, which threw open to Catholic exegesis new avenues of study and made possible renewed research.[27]

Aquinas explains the relationship between causes of different levels: The causes of the same effect are beings of different types. For instance, when I write a text with a pen, the text is written by me

---

[26] Ibid.

[27] Augustine Cardinal Bea, *The Way to Unity After the Council* (London: Geoffrey Chapman, 1967), 92.

and the pen: Both the pen and I are causes of the written text, simultaneously but at different levels. This is what Aquinas said:

> Some find it difficult to understand how natural effects are attributable at once to God and to a natural agent. . . . The power of a lower agent depends on the power of the superior agent, according as the superior agent gives this power to the lower agent whereby it may act; or preserves it; or even applies it to the action, as the artisan applies an instrument to its proper effect, though he neither gives the form whereby the instrument works, nor preserves it, but simply gives it motion. . . . So, just as it is not unfitting for one action to be produced by an agent and its power, so it is not inappropriate for the same effect to be produced by a lower agent and God: by both immediately, though in different ways.[28]

In an action caused by two agents, if both would have the same kind of being—like two men—neither of them would be the cause of the whole effect at his own level. But if an action is caused by two agents who are different kinds of beings, then each causes completely the whole action (as both my pen and I myself write the whole text):

> When the same effect is attributed to a natural cause and to the divine power, it is not as though the effect were produced partly by God and partly by the natural agent: but the whole effect is produced by both, though in different ways, as the same effect is attributed wholly to the instrument, and wholly also to the principal agent.[29]

The reason why God acts through created causes is not that he would not be able to act without them, of course. In the case in which these causes are human, they are more than inanimate instruments, and God grants them some resemblance to divine causation, because of his love:

[28] *Summa contra Gentiles,* Book III, chap. 70.
[29] Ibid.

> Though a natural thing produces its own effect, it is not superfluous for God to produce it, because the natural thing does not produce it except in the power of God. Nor is it superfluous, while God can of Himself produce all natural effects, for them to be produced by other causes: this is not from the insufficiency of God's power, but from the immensity of His goodness, whereby He has wished to communicate His likeness to creatures, not only in point of their being, but likewise in point of their being causes of other things.[30]

Aquinas, being a teacher, uses a pedagogical metaphor to show how divine causality relates to us:

> God so governs things that He makes some of them to be causes of others in government; as a master, who not only imparts knowledge to his pupils, but gives also the faculty of teaching others.[31]

Thomas proposes a general metaphysical scheme, which he applies to all actions. This scheme can be used to understand how both God and human beings can be completely the authors of the Bible, because God chooses such means. The human authors have an impact on the text, as my text will be red if I use a red pen.[32] Thanks to that scheme, there is no need whatsoever to choose between fundamentalism and liberalism: both attitudes are radically non-Catholic. The same scheme explains how the sacraments can be caused both by God and by a human minister.

How do we know what the Bible is?

Who tells us that all these different texts must be together and, in addition, are inspired by the Holy Spirit?

Contemporary Christians can think that the Bible is obviously the Bible. But for centuries, the composition and the content of the

---

30 Ibid.

31 *ST* Ia, q.103, a.6.

32 The example only shows that two causes can cause one effect, not that the biblical text is a text in all ways similar to any text.

Old Testament, in Judaism, were not a matter of easy agreement. As for the content of what we now call the New Testament, some early Christian communities received in their liturgies—as Word of God—some texts that later would not be received as "canonical" (e.g., the letter of Pope St. Clement, written toward the end of the first century), and other communities did not receive some texts that now are canonical (e.g., the second and third letters of John or the Book of Revelation). The need appeared among Christians as it had appeared among Jews to say what the content of the Bible actually is. Some early lists have been found, like the "Muratori fragment," which could be a late second-century text; some local Councils published official lists, like the Council of Rome (382) or the Councils of Hippo (393) and Carthage (397). Most important are the lists of the Council of Florence (1442) and above all of the Council of Trent (1546). There is divergence between Catholics and other Christians about the inclusion of some books in the Old Testament (e.g., the Book of Maccabees), but there is no divergence among the main Christian denominations about the content of the New Testament.

This whole question of canonicity highlights the role of the Church. As St. Augustine said,

> I would not believe in the Gospel if the authority of the Catholic Church did not move me to that.[33]

The Reformers rejected what they perceived as an undue dependence of Scripture upon Church authority "to subject the oracles of God in this way to men's judgment." [34] Calvin considered the Bible to be recognized as the Word of God thanks to its clarity:

---

[33] "Ego vero evangelio non crederem, nisi me catholicae ecclesiae commoveret auctoritas." Augustine, *Contra Epistulam Fundamenti,* cap. V, CSEL 25, 197, ll.22–23. (My translation.)

[34] John Calvin, *Institutes of the Christian Religion,* 4th ed. (Philadelphia/London: The Westminster Press/S.C.M. Press, 1967), IV.IX.14, 1178–79.

> As to their question—How can we be assured that this has sprung from God unless we have recourse to the decree of the Church?—it is as if someone asked: Whence will we learn to distinguish light from darkness, white from black, sweet from bitter? Indeed, Scripture exhibits fully as clear evidence of its own truth as white and black things of their color, or sweet and bitter do of their taste.[35]

The French bishop Jacques-Bénigne Bossuet (1627–1704), however, said it had been an illusion to believe that the divine character of biblical texts would be evident:

> They had gone too far in the confession of faith, when they said about the holy books that one knew them as canonical not so much due to the acceptance by the Church, but through the interior testimony and persuading action of the Holy Spirit. It seems that the ministers now notice that it was an illusion, and that there was no appearance that the faithful with their interior taste, and without any help of the Tradition, would be able to discern the Song of Songs from a profane book, or to feel the divinity of the first books of Genesis, and so on.[36]

To say it with other words: Without the Church and the Tradition of the Church, nobody will know, and know with certainty, that a given group of texts is the Word of God. From the start, the New Testament is part of the primitive tradition, and it is not the first part of that tradition that appeared. These texts were written in and for the Church, which already fully existed. They are addressed to Christian communities (this is explicitly the case for all the Pauline epistles); they use some elements of Christian liturgies (some hymns of Paul or of the Book of Revelation). The New

[35] Ibid., I.VII.2, 76.

[36] Jacques-Bénigne Bossuet, *Histoire des variations des Églises protestantes,* 2 volumes (Paris: Chez la Veuve de Sébastien Mabre-Cramoisy, Imprimeur du Roy, 1688), Vol. II, Book XV, chapter CXIV, 601–2. (My translation.)

Testament in itself is not understandable outside of the Church. A 1963 ecumenical meeting of the Faith and Order Commission of the World Council of Churches (then mainly constituted of Protestants, with some Orthodox)[37] published a text on *Tradition, tradition and traditions* that acknowledged the traditional character of the Bible. The text explains how some documents were used to witness to the apostolic faith, for instance in cases of disagreements:

> These questions imply the search for a criterion. This has been a main concern for the Church since its beginning. In the New Testament we find warnings against false teaching and deviations from the truth of the Gospel. For the post-apostolic Church the appeal to the Tradition received from the apostles became the criterion. As this Tradition was embodied in the apostolic writings, it became natural to use those writings as an authority for determining where the true Tradition was to be found. In the midst of all tradition, these early records of divine revelation have a special basic value, because of their apostolic character. But the Gnostic crisis in the second century shows that the mere existence of apostolic writings did not solve the problem. The question of interpretation arose as soon as the appeal to written documents made its appearance. When the canon of the New Testament had been finally defined and recognized by the Church, it was still more natural to use this body of writings as an indispensable criterion.[38]

[37] Faith and Order is an ecumenical movement founded in 1927 for theological reflection on Christian unity. It merged in 1948 into the World Council of Churches (at its foundation). It retains some internal autonomy. Since 1968, the Roman Catholic Church is a full member of Faith and Order.

[38] *The Fourth World Conference on Faith and Order, Montreal 1963,* ed. P. C. Rodger, Executive Secretary, Commission on Faith and Order, World Council of Churches, and Lukas Vischer, Research Secretary, Commission on Faith and Order, World Council of Churches (New York: Association Press, 1964), §49. From now on text will be quoted with the reference "Montreal 1963," followed by paragraph numbers.

Without the Church, and the Church present through the centuries, nobody would be able to say in the third millennium after Christ what the Bible is. The Bible arose in the Church and for the Church. What this means about its reading and its interpretation will be part of Chapter Four.

SUMMARY

Divine revelation has not been given only to a small group of people at a given place and at a given time. It has been given so that all human beings of all times might be united to God in eternal life (provided they accept it). For that very reason, God also has provided some means so that his infinite gift would not be lost or altered by his versatile human creatures.

For the diffusion of his Good News, Jesus sends his apostles, who preach, show Christ in their life, establish institutions, and supervise the redaction of what would be the New Testament. As their ministry—except for what is properly foundational—remains necessary, the apostles appoint successors: the bishops. The bishops therefore also preach and supervise the preaching, as well as establish and maintain institutions for the diffusion of the Gospel and the celebration of the life-giving sacraments. Through these institutions people of all times discover their vocation to holiness and receive divine helps on that path.

The apostles and others with them wrote the New Testament, as a help given to the already living Church. The Holy Spirit is the author of the Bible, which also has human authors. God and men can be fully authors of the same texts, but at two different levels: the human authors are instruments of God, in the full use of their human skills. Human authorship implies the limited knowledge of the authors and of their culture. Aquinas helps us understand how the same work can have two causes that both accomplish 100% of the effect: metaphysical distinctions make it possible for us to understand how divine action and human action do not have to be opposed to each other in the writing of the Bible (avoiding a necessary choice between fundamentalism and liberalism). These distinctions also explain, for example, how both God and a human minister can work "together" in the sacraments. Without the Church, nobody would know what the Bible is, either in regard to its content or to its nature (i.e. that it is the Word of God).

CHAPTER FOUR

First Condition for a Human Response: Faith Has to be Preached

THIS CHAPTER develops one aspect of the previous one: faith has to be preached. How can people who live two millennia after Jesus Christ believe in him and know that they really believe in him?

Vatican II says that "through this revelation . . . the invisible God out of the abundance of His love speaks to men as friends and lives among them, so that He may invite and take them into fellowship with Himself."[1]

God thus takes the initiative of a dialogue with us, in which he invites us to be with him. A dialogue implies a response of the other partner. Otherwise, there is only a monologue. There are several conditions for our reply to God. Since nobody is Christian by birth, the first condition is that divine revelation has to be announced to people, so that they might have the opportunity to take part in the dialogue with God. As St. Paul says:

> How, then, can they call on the one they have not believed in? And how can they believe in the one of whom they have not heard? And how can they hear without someone preaching to them? And how can they preach unless they are sent?[2]

[1] *Dei Verbum,* §2.
[2] Romans 10:14–15.

The question arises: How can we know that and what God reveals? As Arthur Schopenhauer (1788–1860) says:

> To the people, morals are founded upon theology, as the will expressed by God. . . . Certainly no more efficient foundation of morals can be thought of than the theological one: who would be so presumptuous as to resist the will of the Omnipotent and All-knowing? Certainly nobody; if only this same will would be proclaimed in an absolutely authentic way, open to no doubt. But this is the condition that is never fulfilled.[3]

This chapter will try to show how the preliminary condition of our reply to God (in faith) is made possible.

CONDITIONS OF FAITH FOR ST. THOMAS

In a very precise and synthetic text, Aquinas shows the conditions under which someone might have faith in what God reveals to him:

> Two things are requisite for faith. First, that the things which are of faith should be proposed to man: this is necessary in order that man believe anything explicitly. The second thing requisite for faith is the assent of the believer to the things which are proposed to him.[4]

For example, one of the most central points of Christian faith is that Jesus Christ is true God and true man. Nobody can say this explicitly if he has not first heard about it. And of course to say it is not yet to believe it: one can accept this statement as true, or deny it.

Thomas develops his presentation of the conditions of faith, explaining the interpenetration of divine work and of human work in proclaiming faith. I will mention later the conditions for human assent.

---

[3] Arthur Schopenhauer, "Preischrift über die Grundlage der Moral," §2, *Sämtliche Werke,* Bd. 4 (Leipzig: Brockhaus, 1938), 111–12. (My translation.)

[4] *ST* IIa IIae, q.6, a.1.

> Accordingly, as regards the first of these, faith must needs be from God. Because those things which are of faith surpass human reason, hence they do not come to man's knowledge, unless God reveal them. To some, indeed, they are revealed by God immediately, as those things which were revealed to the apostles and prophets, while to some they are proposed by God in sending preachers of the faith, according to Rm. 10:15: "How shall they preach, unless they be sent?"[5]

What we believe must come from God (divine revelation). If we look at the New Testament, we see that God does not simply communicate directly with everybody, but sends messengers. The Son Incarnate sends apostles who themselves appoint successors, as we saw in the previous chapter.

The trouble for contemporary Christians—it was already a problem in the second century—is to know whether the people who announce the Gospel do really proclaim what God wants us to receive, or something else. In fact, such a concern is already expressed in the New Testament:

> As we have already said, so now I say again: If anybody is preaching to you a gospel other than what you accepted, let him be eternally condemned![6]

The question is especially burning nowadays, and appeared very clearly in the missionary activities of the nineteenth to early twentieth centuries. The 1910 Missionary Conference of Edinburgh was confronted with the obvious difficulty of preaching Christ to non-Christians, inviting them at the same time to become Lutheran rather than Anglican, or Reformed rather than Catholic, or Catholic rather than Methodist. Even though contemporary "ecumenical Christians" try to avoid some of that competition, the fact remains that Christians themselves suggest some doubt about at least part of what other Christians proclaim. In

[5] Ibid.

[6] Galatians 1:9.

contemporary society, most people are immediately confronted with believers of various Christian denominations and various religions. Whom should they believe? I leave aside here the differences among different religions (which would be a topic for another book). Even among people who believe that Jesus Christ is the Revelation of the only God, being himself God and man, there are very significant differences in understanding Christian faith. To take but a few examples of questions on which Christians diverge: What happens in the Eucharist? What is the role of the Bible in Christian faith and in Christian life? Is it necessary to be baptized, and when? If such questions are quite obvious nowadays, they are not new. I will present some positions on this point.

CONDITIONS OF PREACHING AND CHURCH AUTHORITY

Dominican Cardinal Cajetan (Thomas De Vio, 1469–1534) was one of the most prominent theological disciples of St. Thomas Aquinas. He also met Luther at Augsburg in 1518. His commentary on the conditions of faith as presented by Aquinas is worth reading. His starting point is the fact that, beginning with the apostles, faith has to be proclaimed by human beings (or angels), and they might make mistakes:

> As far as faith can depend on a created cause, it can have a created rule. Obviously, two things interact in faith . . . namely [first] the assent and [second] the proposition and explanation of the things which must be believed; from the point of view of the assent, faith depends only on God as agent, object, end, and rule. But from the point of view of the proposition of the things to be believed, it can depend on angels and human beings, through whom God proposes this or that to be believed; from this point of view, "faith comes from hearing the word of God," as Rom. 10 says.[7]

[7] Cajetan, *In Summ. Theol.*, IIa IIae, q.1, a.1, no. X, Sancti Thomae Aquinatis Doctoris Angelici *Opera omnia*, Iussu impensaque Leonis XIII

As we saw in Chapter Three, God knows that some errors might happen in preaching. For the very reason why he revealed himself, he provides the Church with some means to avoid losing that most precious revelation. Cajetan explains what these means are:

> And so that no error might appear in the proposal or explanation of things to be believed, the Holy Spirit provided a created rule, which is the sense and the doctrine of the Church, so that the authority of the Church is the infallible rule of the proposition and explanation of things which must be believed by faith. Therefore, two infallible rules concur in faith, namely divine revelation and the authority of the Church; there is between them this difference: divine revelation is the formal reason of the object of faith, and the authority of the Church is the minister of the object of faith.[8]

These two rules of preaching are divine revelation and Church authority. Divine revelation is called the "formal reason" of faith, namely the reason we believe something. For instance, I believe that Jesus Christ is true God and true man. The reason why I believe this is not my personal opinion; it is divine revelation. This is what Jesus says to Peter when the question of his identity is raised:

> When Jesus came to the region of Caesarea Philippi, he asked his disciples, "Who do people say the Son of Man is?" They replied, "Some say John the Baptist; others say Elijah; and still others, Jeremiah or one of the prophets." "But what about you?" he asked. "Who do you say I am?" Simon Peter answered, "You are the Christ, the Son of the living God." Jesus replied, "Blessed are you, Simon son of Jonah, for this was not revealed to you by man [by flesh and blood], but by my Father in heaven."[9]

P. M. edita, vol. 8 (Rome: Ex Typographia Polyglotta S. C. De Propaganda Fide, 1895), 5. (My translation.)

[8] Ibid.

[9] Matthew 16:13–17.

Divine revelation is thus the reason without which there would be no reason to have faith. The second reason is just an instrument of the first one: faith comes to us through preaching, and the authority of the Church is the reference of true preaching. If two incompatible teachings are proposed for our acceptance, the way of knowing which one is part of divine revelation is the authority of the Church.

Now, what is that Church authority going to be? History shows that it is composed of personal and synodal elements: the bishops gather in local and ecumenical councils. History also shows that divergences sometimes happen among different bishops, among different local councils. What can individual Christians do, then? Another Dominican commentator on St. Thomas Aquinas, John of St. Thomas (1589–1644), explains that in cases of doctrinal differences, since in such circumstances people by definition disagree (e.g., about the meaning of some biblical texts), it is not possible for everyone to be a "final" judge. What is needed, when the point at stake is important, is a sure determination, because otherwise even the Bible becomes useless:

> Everybody cannot declare in a way that would resolve the question by a determination, and infallibly so, because of the mere fact that there is the whole controversy about whether what the Church proposes and declares is contained in Scripture, and the fact that some deny it and others affirm it; therefore if everyone could declare on that, everyone would pronounce for himself, and all would stay within the same confusion; therefore it is necessary that the declaration and proposition by the Church be without any suspicion and fallibility; otherwise we would always have a doubt on whether this is contained in Scripture.[10]

[10] John of St. Thomas, In Iam, q. 1, disp. I, art. 3, Ioannes a Sancto Thoma, *Cursus theologicus,* In Summam theologicam D. Thomae, Nova editio, Tomus primus, in Primae Partis Quaestiones I–VII (Paris: Vivès, 1883), 433. (My translation.)

He takes into consideration that authority could belong to a group of bishops. But that does not seem to be the ultimate system:

> If it were said that the authority and the supreme power about things of faith be divided among several persons, like several archbishops or primates, this would absolutely imply that by the fact itself that one of them would determine some proposition about faith, if he would have about it an infallible authority, not only his subjects but also all the faithful, i.e. also the subjects of the other archbishops, would have to accept that determination, since it would be infallible and because faith must be one for all. . . . If all these supreme powers would have to agree in the same way on what belongs to the substance of religion, and if they would have to govern in the same way, since otherwise if one would act differently from the other, the unity of faith and the religion of the Church would perish, this would be done far better by one.[11]

Following this line of argumentation, the First Vatican Council (1870) expresses the link between faith and the Magisterium in terms more polemical than the ones usually used nowadays:

> Everybody knows that those heresies, condemned by the fathers of Trent, which rejected the divine Magisterium of the Church and allowed religious questions to be a matter for the judgment of each individual, have gradually collapsed into a multiplicity of sects, either at variance or in agreement with one another; and by this means a good many people have had all faith in Christ destroyed. Indeed even the Holy Bible itself, which they at one time claimed to be the sole source and judge of the Christian faith, is no longer held to be divine, but they begin to assimilate it to the inventions of myth.[12]

---

[11] Ibid., In IIam–IIae, q.1–7, disp. I, art.3 , in the same edition, Tomus septimus, in Secundam Secundae . . . , 1886, 184–85. (My translation.)

[12] Vatican Council I, Dogmatic Constitution on the Catholic Faith, *Dei Filius,* Introduction, *Decrees of the Ecumenical Councils: Trent to Vatican II,* ed. Norman P. Tanner S.J., vol. 2 (London: Sheed & Ward, 1990), vol. 804.

The Council affirms the primacy of the pope as means of safeguarding the unity among bishops, in a way similar to the ministry of Peter among the apostles:

> In order, then, that the episcopal office should be one and undivided and that, by the union of the clergy, the whole multitude of believers should be held together in the unity of faith and communion, he set blessed Peter over the rest of the apostles and instituted in him the permanent principle of both unities and their visible foundation.[13]

The same teaching will be repeated by Vatican II, although there with a stronger insistence on all bishops being a college:

> Jesus Christ, the eternal Shepherd, established His Holy Church, having sent forth the apostles as He Himself had been sent by the Father; and He willed that their successors, namely the bishops, should be shepherds in His Church even to the consummation of the world. And in order that the episcopate itself might be one and undivided, He placed Blessed Peter over the other apostles, and instituted in him a permanent and visible source and foundation of unity of faith and communion. And all this teaching about the institution, the perpetuity, the meaning and reason for the sacred primacy of the Roman Pontiff and of his infallible magisterium, this Sacred Council again proposes to be firmly believed by all the faithful.[14]

Of course the pope does not rule the Church alone: he does it with the other bishops, as this is best expressed in the gathering of Ecumenical Councils. But such Councils do not have an authority in themselves, if they are not approved by the pope:

> The college or body of bishops has no authority unless it is understood together with the Roman Pontiff, the successor of Peter as its head. . . . A council is never ecumenical unless it is confirmed

[13] Ibid., *Pastor Aeternus,* Introduction, 811–12.
[14] *Lumen Gentium,* §18.

> or at least accepted as such by the successor of Peter; and it is prerogative of the Roman Pontiff to convoke these councils, to preside over them and to confirm them.[15]

The whole reasoning of this section is expressed in his own terms by the Russian philosopher and theologian Vladimir Soloviov (1853–1900), whose starting point is the necessity of Church unity and the idea that biblical texts should not remain without effect:

> The terrestrial Church, which was to enter the current of history and to undergo ceaseless changes and variations in circumstances and in her external relations, needed, to maintain her identity, a power which would be essentially conservative and yet creative, inalterable in the essentials and flexible in the forms; finally, the terrestrial Church, intended to act and to affirm herself against all the powers of evil in the middle of a formless humanity, was to be provided a point of absolutely firm and irrefragable support, stronger than the gates of hell. —And we know, on the one hand, that Christ envisaged this need for ecclesiastical monarchy while conferring on only one the supreme and indivisible power of her Church; and we see, on another side, that, of all the ecclesiastical capacities of the Christian world, there is one which maintains perpetually and invariably its central and universal character and which, at the same time, by a tradition old and general, is especially attached to what Christ said: "You are Peter, and upon this rock I will build my Church," and: "The gates of hell will not prevail against her". The word of Christ could not remain without effect in Christian history; and the principal phenomenon of this history was to have a sufficient cause in the Word of God. Let one find for us, for the word of Christ with Peter, a corresponding effect other than the chair of Peter, and let one find for us, for this chair, a sufficient cause other than the promise made to Peter.[16]

---

15 Ibid., §22.

16 Vladimir Soloviev, "La Russie et l'Église universelle," *La Sophia et les autres écrits français* (Lausanne: La Cité/L'Age d'Homme, 1978), 208. (My translation.)

So that faith could be proclaimed and received with certainty, God provided human rules for a preaching that he wanted to be human. Without such human rules, the reading of the Bible itself might become so doubtful that an act of faith would be impossible.

Does such a statement make ecumenical dialogue difficult? I think it rather makes it possible and meaningful. This is going to be the next point.

ECUMENISM LOOKS FOR UNITY IN FAITH

The already mentioned 1963 Assembly of Faith and Order in Montreal published part of its final document under the title *Tradition, tradition and traditions.* The fact that a text prepared mainly by Protestant theologians addressed the question of Tradition implies that the fact itself had to be justified. From the time of the Reformation, a certain opposition to an authoritative use of tradition in theology had been a trademark of Protestantism. The Montreal assembly gives a definition of what is meant by "tradition," distinguishing three meanings of the word:

> In our report we have distinguished between a number of different meanings of the word tradition. We speak of the Tradition (with a capital T), tradition (with a small t) and traditions. By the Tradition is meant the Gospel itself, transmitted from generation to generation in and by the Church, Christ himself present in the life of the Church. By tradition is meant the traditionary process. The term traditions is used in two senses, to indicate both the diversity of forms of expression and also what we call confessional traditions, for instance the Lutheran tradition or the Reformed tradition. In the latter part of our report the word appears in a further sense, when we speak of cultural traditions.[17]

The main meaning of the word is then Tradition, understood in a way very similar to the text on Revelation published two

[17] Montreal 1963, §39.

years later by Vatican II: transmission of Revelation.[18] The "traditionary process" means a specific way of communication: in all fields of knowledge, something can be discovered, explained a first time, or transmitted by way of tradition (there are traditions of medicine, cuisine, mountain climbing . . .). Then, there are different traditions within Christianity, both within the same church and among different Christian denominations.

Two things are remarkable in the Montreal document, at least for my present purpose. The first is that an ecumenical text written without active Catholic collaboration (but with an Orthodox and Anglican collaboration) explains why it is necessary to overcome divisions among Christians about Tradition, or why it is not really possible to be Christian without a tradition:

> For a variety of reasons, it has now become necessary to reconsider these positions. We are more aware of our living in various confessional traditions, e.g. that stated paradoxically in the saying: "It has been the tradition of my church not to attribute any weight to tradition." Historical study and not least the encounter of the churches in the ecumenical movement have led us to realize that the proclamation of the Gospel is always inevitably historically conditioned. We are also aware that in Roman Catholic theology the concept of tradition is undergoing serious reconsideration.[19]

In fact all Christians are part of a tradition. The ecumenical movement itself makes it impossible to ignore the existence of different Christian identities and the historical element in them, because different meanings given to words or sentences cannot be understood without some knowledge of the historical context, both past and present. On top of that, since "the Church is sent by Christ to proclaim the Gospel to all men, the Tradition must be handed on in time and also in space;"[20] "it is necessary that again

[18] *Dei Verbum.*
[19] Montreal 1963, §44.
[20] Ibid., §64.

the essential content should find expression in terms of new cultures," [21] where Scripture cannot simply be repeated without interpretation. More than that: "A mere reiteration of the words of Holy Scripture would be a betrayal of the Gospel which has to be made understandable and has to convey a challenge to the world." [22]

Up to a certain point, all Christians share a common Tradition:

> Our starting-point is that we are all living in a tradition which goes back to our Lord and has its roots in the Old Testament, and are all indebted to that tradition inasmuch as we have received the revealed truth, the Gospel, through its being transmitted from one generation to another.[23]

Still, there are different traditions, above all different denominations. They can have different legitimate expressions of the same faith, but on some points they can also contradict each other. To take but one example: Is the Eucharist an actualization of the sacrifice of the Cross, that has to be celebrated by a bishop or by a priest ordained by a bishop? Montreal expresses the problem:

> Is it possible to determine more precisely what the content of the one Tradition is, and by what means? Do all traditions which claim to be Christian contain the Tradition? How can we distinguish between traditions embodying the true Tradition and merely human traditions? Where do we find the genuine Tradition, and where impoverished tradition or even distortion of tradition? Tradition can be a faithful transmission of the Gospel, but also a distortion of it.[24]

The text then goes on looking for a solution to that problem, which is as old as the Church:

---

[21] Ibid., §66.
[22] Ibid., §50.
[23] Ibid., §45.
[24] Ibid., §48.

> These questions imply the search for a criterion. This has been a main concern for the Church since its beginning.[25]

The document gives a list of criteria. On some, more or less all Christians would agree: fidelity to Christ was first secured by apostolic authority, then thanks to apostolic texts that were recognized and defined as the Canon of the New Testament.[26] But of course the New Testament must be interpreted, and the question takes a new turn:

> The necessity of interpretation raises again the question of the criterion for the genuine Tradition. Throughout the history of the Church the criterion has been sought in the Holy Scriptures rightly interpreted. But what is "right interpretation"?[27]

Everybody would agree that the correct interpretation is the one guided by the Holy Spirit, but different interpretations can all claim to receive such a guidance.[28] Different criteria have been used through history, combined in different ways: interpretation of some biblical text in the light of the whole Bible or of a central point of Scripture; central importance of one specific message or of the individual conscience; reference to the Ecumenical Councils, to the Fathers of the Church, to the Magisterium.[29] The list itself shows both the necessity of a solution and some diversity about what the solution could be. The Montreal assembly acknowledges a very important point: these criteria do not mean that the Bible is submitted to an external criterion, but that the interpretations of the Bible need such a criterion:

> In none of these cases where the principle of interpretation is found elsewhere than in Scripture is the authority thought to be

[25] Ibid., §49.
[26] Cf. ibid.
[27] Cf. ibid., §51.
[28] Cf. ibid., §52.
[29] Cf. ibid., §53.

> alien to the central concept of Holy Scripture. On the contrary, it is considered as providing just a key to the understanding of what is said in Scripture.[30]

Even though "[m]odern biblical scholarship has already done much to bring the different churches together by conducting them towards the Tradition,"[31] some differences remain. These differences are due in part to the different presuppositions in biblical scholarship itself. The Montreal assembly could not find the desired criterion. Thirty-five years later a study group mandated by the same commission of Faith and Order published a new document on the same question.[32] This new text rightly praises the Montreal assembly for what it achieved, but also notes that the World Conference could not find a solution to the correctly identified problem:

> Montreal thereby helped the churches to begin to realize that the one Tradition is witnessed to in Scripture and transmitted by the Holy Spirit through the Church. This means the canon of Scripture came into being within the Tradition, which finds expression within the various traditions of the Church. In this way Montreal helped to overcome the old contrast between "sola Scriptura" and "Scripture and tradition" and to show that the different hermeneutical criteria in the different traditions belong together. The ongoing interaction between Tradition and traditions enables faithful transmission, even though from time to time there have been distortions of the apostolic faith. But Montreal did not fully explain what it means that the one Tradition is embodied in concrete traditions and cultures. . . . It must be recognized that Montreal left open the vital question of how churches can discern the one Tradition.[33]

---

[30] Ibid.

[31] Ibid., §55.

[32] Faith and Order, *A Treasure in Earthen Vessels, An Instrument for an Ecumenical Reflection on Hermeneutics,* Faith and Order Paper, No. 182 (Geneva: WCC Publications, 1998).

[33] Ibid., §§16–18.

It seems to me that this more recent document does not solve the question either. It summarizes dialogues on questions such as authority, the method of dialogue, the role of scholarship, a holistic reading, and moral criteria. But all these useful criteria are not sufficient to solve the question of possibly incompatible readings of Scripture.

In 2005, the French ecumenical Groupe des Dombes published a document on authority in the Church. Once again, the question is: How is it possible to declare that Christians are united? The document mentions the normal decision-making process in Protestant churches and some of its difficulties:

> On the Protestant side, synods are the normal way of exercising doctrinal authority. They gather regularly and have a full deliberative voice. Decisions taken by these synods bind only the Churches who called them, which makes a supranational decision very difficult. On top of that, decisions can be discussed by a succeeding synod, which makes a lasting decision difficult. One must also mention the considerable question of the representativeness of the delegates to the synod.[34]

The same text adds that the reception of ecumenical agreements would imply some authority[35] and that therefore Protestant churches should develop some stronger authority structures:

> We ask the Churches of the Reformation to develop new processes of decision making, beyond regional and national Churches, within large denominational organizations. . . . It matters for the testimony to be given to the Gospel in the world that Churches can visibly manifest their doctrinal communion and decide together on the highest possible number of matters.[36]

34 Groupe des Dombes, "Un seul maître," *L'autorité doctrinale dans l'Église* (Paris: Bayard, 2005), §392. (My translation.)

35 Cf. ibid., §440.

36 Ibid., §463 (my translation). The text also says that it would be good for elements of synodality to be developed in the Catholic Church (diocesan

The question is therefore always the same: How is it possible to declare that Christians of different denominations from a certain time on share the same faith on a point that used to divide them? If no answer can be given to that question, the whole ecumenical project becomes more or less meaningless.

George Lindbeck, an American Lutheran theologian (and an observer at Vatican II), insists on the necessity of infallibility for ecumenism. The Catholic tradition is not the only one to presuppose some kind of infallibility:

> That church seems permanently committed to a principle of dogmatic infallibility which excludes the possibility of admitting that popes and councils have ever erred in such a way as to justify a protest like the Protestant one. Indeed, the very self-identity of Rome seems to depend on its maintaining this conviction. And, conversely, the self-identity of Protestantism depends on its insistence that the Reformation break in the unity of the church, despite its tragedy, was legitimate and necessary in faithfulness to the gospel.[37]

When Hans Küng criticized the Catholic understanding of infallibility, Lindbeck supported the negative reaction of Catholic bishops, saying that a strict denial of infallibility would make impossible any confession of Christian faith:

> It is his first premise which troubles me, and for much the same reasons that it has troubled many Catholics. The German bishops concentrate on this in their statement on Küng's book, and it is also the problem which chiefly disturbs Rahner amid all his other questions about Küng's procedure. Is it really the case that all true propositions can become infected with error, with falsehood?

synods, episcopal conferences, Synod of Bishops . . .), cf. ibid., §§457–59.

[37] George A. Lindbeck, *The Future of Roman Catholic Theology: Vatican II—Catalyst for Change* (Philadelphia: Fortress Press, 1970), 94.

> Above all, does this hold for all religious statements, for all affirmations of Christian faith, for all—not just some—dogmas? Is it true, for example, of "Jesus is Lord"?[38]

Indeed all religions need some infallibility,[39] and Christianity more than all others.[40] It is especially required for Christian unity, at least if unity is understood as a real one:

> Clearly such a position depends, as we have already said, on a high estimate of the importance of the Church's visible unity. It involves the conviction that God wills unity, not only "wishfully" or "eschatologically," but with present and enduring efficacity.[41]

Infallibility is necessary to Christian unity because of the past and present situation of division. All present Christians live with some convictions about other Christians, and on some points unity would require them to revise some of their present convictions, either because they are not precise, or because they should admit other expressions of the same contents, or simply because they are wrong. Such revisions are not superficial: they can go

---

[38] George A. Lindbeck, "The Infallibility Debate," *The Infallibility Debate,* ed. John J. Kirvan (New York: Paulist Press, 1971), 111.

[39] Cf. ibid., 116–17: "What then should be said about infallible propositions from a religious perspective? It would seem that the case against them collapses. There are the strongest possible religious reasons for insisting, not only on the possibility, but on the actuality, of infallible affirmations. This, as we shall see, does not necessarily mean that the Roman Catholic or any other magisterium is infallible. What we are talking about is the inevitability of infallibility, not only for Catholicism, but for Protestantism, not only for Christianity, but also for non-Christian religions."

[40] Cf. ibid., 120: "Of all religions, however, Christianity is the most absolutely—or outrageously—infallibilist, and therefore the one least capable of surrendering the notion of infallible dogmas. It alone affirms that the God who is ultimate reality and truth has fully and definitively communicated himself for us men and our salvation in an historically locatable and empirically tangible person, Jesus."

[41] Ibid., 149.

against a conviction deeply rooted in people's conscience. The only way to overcome such an inner crisis would be no less than some divine authority:

> If this unity is in addition regarded as an ultimate value, an irrevocable gift of God whose loss is unthinkable, then, in a Christian context, the final adjudicator of controversies must be infallible, must be divinely protected against final error, even if not against preliminary falsity. This is necessary because otherwise believers would sometimes not be able in good conscience to remain in the Church when it decided against them.[42]

A very obvious problem appears: Even granted that Christian unity requires some infallible authority, one reason Christians are divided is precisely that they do not agree on what such an authority might be. As far as I know, the only ecumenical dialogue where some infallible authority was agreed on in precise terms was the Anglican-Roman Catholic International Commission (ARCIC) dialogue, in its 1998 document *The Gift of Authority*.[43] The Commission is confident that Christ helps his Church so that she will be able in every age to give him a response of faith:

> In every age Christians have said "Amen" to Christ's promise that the Spirit will guide his Church into all truth. The New Testament frequently echoes this promise by referring to the boldness, assurance and certainty to which Christians can lay claim (cf. Lk 1.4; 1 Thess 2.2; Eph 3.2; Heb 11.1). In their concern to make the Gospel accessible to all who are open to receive it, those charged with the ministry of memory and teaching have accepted new and hitherto unfamiliar expressions of faith. Some of these formula-

---

42 Ibid.

43 Anglican-Roman Catholic International Commission (ARCIC II), *The Gift of Authority: Authority in the Church III, An agreed statement by the [second] Anglican-Roman Catholic International Commission* (London: CTS, 1999).

tions have initially generated doubt and disagreement about their fidelity to the apostolic Tradition. In the process of testing such formulations, the Church has moved cautiously, but with confidence in the promise of Christ that it will persevere and be maintained in the truth (cf. Mt 16.18; Jn 16.13). This is what is meant by the *indefectibility* of the Church.[44]

Authority in the Church is "conciliar, collegial and primatial."[45] ARCIC acknowledges a specific service of the bishop of Rome for the service of the faith of all Christians:

> Within his wider ministry, the Bishop of Rome offers a specific ministry concerning the discernment of truth, as an expression of universal primacy. . . . Such authoritative teaching is a particular exercise of the calling and responsibility of the body of bishops to teach and affirm the faith. When the faith is articulated in this way, the Bishop of Rome proclaims the faith of the local churches. It is thus the wholly reliable teaching of the whole Church that is operative in the judgement of the universal primate. In solemnly formulating such teaching, the universal primate must discern and declare, with the assured assistance and guidance of the Holy Spirit, in fidelity to Scripture and Tradition, the authentic faith of the whole Church, that is, the faith proclaimed from the beginning. It is this faith, the faith of all the baptised in communion, and this only, that each bishop utters with the body of bishops in council. It is this faith which the Bishop of Rome in certain circumstances has a duty to discern and make explicit. This form of authoritative teaching has no stronger guarantee from the Spirit than have the solemn definitions of ecumenical councils. The reception of the primacy of the Bishop of Rome entails the recognition of this specific ministry of the universal primate. We believe that this is a gift to be received by all the churches.[46]

[44] Ibid., §41.
[45] Cf. ibid., §45.
[46] Ibid., §47.

No text signed by an ecumenical commission had ever been so positive about some kind of papal infallibility, understood as a service given to the possibility itself of faith, which presupposes a correct interpretation of Scripture.

After this section, which has shown the search for a criterion of discernment among different Christian traditions, along the lines of a service of authority, I will try to present a Catholic answer to that ecumenical question.

HISTORICAL SCHOLARSHIP AND FAITH

Christianity is a historical religion. The Bible shows a God who reveals himself through history: He gives a promised land; frees his enslaved people; sends his Son who lives, dies, and rises again; and shows his grace changing human lives. Does that mean that historical scholarship would be the right criterion for a discernment among different Christian traditions or different claims to be Christian?

Historical study can certainly help. A better knowledge of the meaning of biblical texts in the context of their original culture helps us understand them, although our reading of the Word of God cannot be reduced to historical research and is not reserved to historians. Some knowledge of Church history is at the very center of what Christians mean by "Tradition": the Church cannot dispense with a reference to Jesus Christ, to the apostles, to early Councils.

Still, history is not enough. To say it in the very concise words of John Henry Newman:

> For myself, I would simply confess that no doctrine of the Church can be rigorously proved by historical evidence: but at the same time that no doctrine can be simply disproved by it.[47]

[47] John Henry Newman, *Certain Difficulties Felt by Anglicans in Catholic Teaching, In a Letter addressed to the Rev. E. B. Pusey, D.D., on occasion of his Eirenicon of 1864; And in a Letter addressed to the Duke of Norfolk, on occasion of Mr. Gladstone's Expostulation of 1874,* Vol. II (London, New York and Bombay: Green, and Co., 1900), 312.

Cardinal Ratzinger says something very similar about the particular case of papal primacy, and calls for a collaboration between history and theology:

> Without doubt, it is true that history as such cannot give any absolute certainty about the truth of faith. . . . Such a collaboration [between history and theology] requires that the question about doctrinal evaluation of historical data be asked in the light of Tradition, as a *locus* and criterion of truth consciousness of ecclesial faith.[48]

For rather similar reasons, John Zizioulas, Orthodox Metropolitan of Pergamon, asks for a theological rather than historical understanding of papal primacy:

> The question for me is not an historical but a theological one. If there is a necessity for the primacy of the Bishop of Rome this could not be because history demands it, for even if history demanded it (which is in my view doubtful, to say the least) it would not make a necessary thing for the Church's *esse*. The same thing would have to be said if the reasons offered for such a primacy were to be practical and utilitarian. For if this were the case the primacy we are considering would not be a matter of the Church's *esse* but of her *bene esse*, and this would be less than satisfactory to a theologian. The primacy of the Bishop of Rome has to be theologically justified or else be ignored altogether.[49]

History is not enough, not only because different historians have different views about the past as they have different views

[48] Joseph Ratzinger, "Discorso in apertura del Simposio," *Il primato del successore di Pietro,* Atti del Simposio teologico, Roma, dicembre 1996, "Atti e Documenti" 7 (Roma: Libreria Editrice Vaticana, 1998), 17–18. (My translation.)

[49] Metropolitan John of Pergamon (Zizioulas), "Primacy in the Church: An Orthodox Approach," *Petrine Ministry and the Unity of the Church: Toward a Patient and Fraternal Dialogue,* ed. James F. Puglisi, S.A. (Collegeville, MN: Michael Glazier, The Liturgical Press, 1999), 123.

about the meaning of some biblical texts, but also because as a human science history cannot reach the level of God (any more than philosophy or biology can):

> How illusory it would be to conclude that we can make use of such a return in order to grasp together all the legitimate development of dogma accomplished during twenty centuries under the prophetic light and the light of theological faith whereby God helps us, and to suppose that we can rediscover, by means of purely human disciplines: archaeology, philology, exegesis, history of religions, contemporary philosophies, the meaning of "things no eye has seen, no ear has heard, no human heart conceived, the welcome God has prepared for those who love him" (1 Cor 2.9).[50]

If Christian unity were to be established on the basis of historical studies, such a unity would be no more than a philosophical unity. Its root would not be divine revelation. After all, even persons who were able to meet Jesus in his earthly life could not recognize his divinity, and when Peter confessed his faith, Jesus told him, "flesh and blood has not revealed this to you, but my Father who is in heaven."[51] When the Apostle Thomas confessed the risen Lord, seeing him face to face, he was saying infinitely more than what he could see (i.e., a living man). People who met Lazarus after his resurrection did not consider him to be God. If some did, they were wrong. Quoting St. Gregory the Great, Aquinas comments on Thomas's confession of faith:

> Thomas "saw one thing, and believed another": he saw the Man, and believing Him to be God, he made profession of his faith, saying: "My Lord and my God."[52]

Faith gives us the possibility of knowing beyond—not against—the capacities of human reason. Human reason could see Jesus as a

[50] Charles Journet, *What Is Dogma?* (London: Burns & Oates, 1964), 56–57.
[51] Matthew 16:17.
[52] *ST* IIa IIae, q.1, a.4, ad 1.

man, rightly so, but not as God. Only faith acknowledges his divinity. History as a human science is within the field of human reason. History can certainly be a help to, but not a substitute for, faith. Collaboration between history and theology, both working honestly with their proper methods, implies that the believer sees in historical events some divine action throughout the whole of history. This is also why Pope Paul VI refused to allow that the Church—which always wants to be increasingly faithful to her apostolic origins—be reduced to a form of the past:

> Let us not deceive ourselves into thinking that the edifice of the Church which has now become large and majestic for the glory of God as His magnificent temple should be reduced to its early minimal proportions as if they alone were true and good.[53]

If history, useful as it is in ecumenical dialogue for a better mutual knowledge, is not a sufficient criterion of discernment among Christian traditions, one must find something else. It seems to me that the specific Catholic contribution to Christian unity can be summarized as "dogma." Before I explain why dogma is an ecumenical contribution, I must clarify the concept of "dogma."

What Dogma Is and What It Is Not

Catholic "dogmas" are often misunderstood by other Christians because they think that Catholics want to extend the definitive revelation in Jesus Christ.

When the Catholic Church proclaims a dogma, the intention is not to introduce a new revelation. Because "the deepest truth about God and the salvation of man shines out for our sake in Christ, who is both the mediator and the fullness of all revelation,"[54] "the Christian dispensation, . . . as the new and definitive covenant, will never pass away and we now await no further new public revelation before

[53] Paul VI, Encyclical *Ecclesiam Suam* (6 August 1964), §47.

[54] *Dei Verbum*, 2.

the glorious manifestation of our Lord Jesus Christ (see 1 Tim 6:14 and Tit 2:13)."[55] The fear of the Reformers that the Church would introduce a new faith[56] is not justified by the official position of the Catholic Church. Dogmas have to be understood as a development of our understanding of the definitive revelation of Jesus Christ:

> The Apostles, handing on what they themselves had received, warn the faithful to hold fast to the traditions which they have learned either by word of mouth or by letter (see 2 Thess 2:15), and to fight in defense of the faith handed on once and for all (see Jude 1:3). Now what was handed on by the Apostles includes everything which contributes toward the holiness of life and increase in faith of the peoples of God; and so the Church, in her teaching, life and worship, perpetuates and hands on to all generations all that she herself is, all that she believes. This tradition which comes from the Apostles develops in the Church with the help of the Holy Spirit. For there is a growth in the understanding of the realities and the words which have been handed down. This happens through the contemplation and study made by believers, who treasure these things in their hearts (see Luke 2:19, 51) through a penetrating understanding of the spiritual realities which they experience, and through the preaching of those who have received through episcopal succession the sure gift of truth. For as the centuries succeed one another, the Church constantly moves forward toward the fullness of divine truth until the words of God reach their complete fulfilment in her.[57]

The deepening of the definitive revelation is not a new thing in the Church. When the first Council of Nicea, in 325, proclaimed most of what is now recognized as the common basic Christian confession of faith—the Creed of Nicea and Constantinople (the first Council of Constantinople, 381, having developed the part concerning the Holy Spirit)—the intention of the Council was

[55] Ibid., §4.

[56] Cf. John Calvin, *Institutes of Christian Religion,* IV.8.9, already quoted.

[57] *Dei Verbum,* §8.

not to express a faith different from the one of the New Testament, but to express the same faith in order to respond to some new questions. Therefore, when Nicea says that the Son is "of one Being *(homoousios, consubstantialis)* with the Father," the intention of this non-biblical word is to express the content of the Bible vis-à-vis the Arians, who used biblical terms against the content of the Bible (denying the divinity of Christ). Ecumenical texts have perfectly accepted the necessity of such a development of formulations for the sake of a continuity in content:

> In order to respond to their calling, churches which belong to different Christian traditions and live in diverse cultural, social, political and religious contexts, need to reappropriate their common basis in the apostolic faith so that they may confess their faith together. In so doing, they will give common witness to the saving purposes of the Triune God for all humanity and all creation. The apostolic faith must always be confessed anew and interpreted in the context of changing times and places: it must be in continuity with the original witness of the apostolic community and with the faithful explication of that witness throughout the ages.[58]
>
> In the primitive Church, the evidence for the development of common expressions of belief is clear. They were used in different settings, in worship, preaching and teaching and particularly in the instruction of candidates for baptism. What is usually known as the Apostles' Creed probably arose in this context. They were also used as a way of defending the faith within the limits of diversity. The Creed of the Council of Nicea in 325 was a response to one such particular crisis. The expression of this text at Constantinople in 381 summarized the faith transmitted by the apostles on behalf of the entire Christian community, with a claim to authority for all Christians in every place.[59]

[58] *Confessing the One Faith: An Ecumenical Explication of the Apostolic Faith as it is Confessed in the Nicene-Constantinopolitan Creed* (381), rev. ed., Faith and Order Paper, No. 153 (Geneva: WCC Publications, 1991), §5.

[59] *Towards Sharing the One Faith: A Study Guide for Discussion Groups,* Faith and Order Paper, No. 173 (Geneva: WCC Publications, 1996), §25.

Not only is the intention of the proclamation of new articles of faith not to proclaim a new faith, but also anything that—even perhaps coming from God—would be new could not be part of faith and would only be a possible help to individuals. The Congregation for the Doctrine of the Faith explains clearly that general doctrine, when it speaks about the mysteries of Fatima:

> The teaching of the Church distinguishes between "public Revelation" and "private revelations." The two realities differ not only in degree but also in essence. The term "public Revelation" refers to the revealing action of God directed to humanity as a whole and which finds its literary expression in the two parts of the Bible. . . . In Christ, God has said everything, that is, he has revealed himself completely, and therefore Revelation came to an end with the fulfilment of the mystery of Christ as enunciated in the New Testament. To explain the finality and completeness of Revelation, the *Catechism of the Catholic Church* quotes a text of Saint John of the Cross: "In giving us his Son, his only Word (for he possesses no other), he spoke everything to us at once in this sole Word—and he has no more to say . . . because what he spoke before to the prophets in parts, he has now spoken all at once by giving us the All Who is His Son. Any person questioning God or desiring some vision or revelation would be guilty not only of foolish behavior but also of offending him, by not fixing his eyes entirely upon Christ and by living with the desire for some other novelty" (No. 65; Saint John of the Cross, *The Ascent of Mount Carmel,* II, 22). . . . In this context, it now becomes possible to understand rightly the concept of "private revelation," which refers to all the visions and revelations which have taken place since the completion of the New Testament. This is the category to which we must assign the message of Fatima. In this respect, let us listen once again to the *Catechism of the Catholic Church*: "Throughout the ages, there have been so-called 'private' revelations, some of which have been recognized by the authority of the Church. . . . It is not their role to complete Christ's definitive Revelation, but to help live more fully by it in a certain period of history" (No. 67). This

> clarifies two things: 1. The authority of private revelations is essentially different from that of the definitive public Revelation. The latter demands faith; in it in fact God himself speaks to us through human words and the mediation of the living community of the Church. . . . 2. Private revelation is a help to this faith, and shows its credibility precisely by leading one back to the definitive public Revelation. . . . Such a message can be a genuine help in understanding the Gospel and living it better at a particular moment in time; therefore it should not be disregarded. It is a help which is offered, but which one is not obliged to use.[60]

Such a teaching can help ecumenical dialogue, because Protestant theologians tend to suspect Catholic theologians of underestimating the definitive character of biblical revelation. Still, these recent texts of the Catholic Magisterium do not express a new development due to an ecumenical mindset. St. Thomas Aquinas already said that in theology only Scripture had a proper authority, because of the definitive revelation:

> Sacred doctrine makes use also of the authority of philosophers in those questions in which they were able to know the truth by natural reason, as Paul quotes a saying of Aratus: "As some also of your own poets said: For we are also His offspring" (Acts 17:28). Nevertheless, sacred doctrine makes use of these authorities as extrinsic and probable arguments; but properly uses the authority of the canonical Scriptures as an incontrovertible proof, and the authority of the doctors of the Church as one that may properly be used, yet merely as probable. For our faith rests upon the revelation made to the apostles and prophets who wrote the canonical books, and not on the revelations (if any such there are) made to other doctors.[61]

---

[60] "Congregation for the Doctrine of the Faith, *The Message of Fatima,* Theological Commentary, 26 June 2000," *Osservatore Romano,* 28 June 2000, VII.

[61] *ST* Ia, q.1, a.8, ad 2.

Thomas added that the point was not to use only the biblical text itself, but to respect its meaning, even when this implies introducing new words:

> Although the word person is not found applied to God in Scripture, either in the Old or New Testament, nevertheless what the word signifies is found to be affirmed of God in many places of Scripture; as that He is the supreme self-subsisting being, and the most perfectly intelligent being. If we could speak of God only in the very terms themselves of Scripture, it would follow that no one could speak about God in any but the original language of the Old or New Testament. The urgency of confuting heretics made it necessary to find new words to express the ancient faith about God.[62]

Not to go astray from the content of Scripture, but to be able to express it also with other words—this is the very meaning of Tradition. And the reason why new expressions are needed is not only that the Bible must be translated, or that we must give an answer to questions asked in new terms, but also that, in any case, any reading of the Bible cannot not be an interpretation. Johann Adam Möhler (1796–1838) expressed this at the most radical level:

> If it is said that Scripture alone is enough for the Christian, one is justified in asking the meaning of this assertion. Scripture alone, apart from our apprehension, is nothing at all; it is a dead letter. Only the product, which comes into light by the direction of our spiritual activities from the Scripture, is something.[63]

It should be clear by now that a dogma is not meant to be a new public revelation, because this is simply impossible: in Christ we have received the fullness of revelation, which we can only deepen until the same Christ comes again in glory. A dogma is

---

[62] *ST* Ia, q.29, a.3, ad 1.

[63] Johann Adam Möhler, *Unity in the Church or The Principle of Catholicism: Presented in the Spirit of the Church Fathers of the First Three Centuries* (Washington, DC: The Catholic University of America Press, 1996), 117.

only an authoritative and binding interpretation of the definitive revelation, also showing what is implicitly contained in it. It is important to stress this aspect, since some non-Catholic Christians reject Catholic dogmas because of what they do not know to be a Catholic principle: No new revelation could happen that would impose anything new to our faith. The point of dogma is only to deepen our knowledge of revelation and to make it certain in cases of doubt. And such cases cannot be avoided, because any reading of the Bible implies an interpretation, and that interpretation can be wrong.

Dogma as a Catholic Contribution to Ecumenism

In matters of faith, the Catholic Church wants certainty. Quite simply, if there is no certainty in faith, either faith is not worth it, or what we are speaking about is not faith.

For Aquinas, one of the main characteristics of faith is its certainty. He acknowledges that, because of the weakness of our capacity for knowledge, faith is not the clearest knowledge. "Science"—that is, a sure human knowledge based on sensitive data rightly interpreted—is more obvious than faith, and in this regard it is more certain:

> Certitude may be considered on the part of the subject, and thus the more a man's intellect lays hold of a thing, the more certain it is. In this way, faith is less certain, because matters of faith are above the human intellect, whereas the objects of the aforesaid three virtues [wisdom, science and understanding] are not.[64]

That faith is not the most obvious human knowledge does not mean that it is not the most certain one in the strongest sense of the term, because of its cause, namely divine Revelation:

---

[64] *ST* IIa IIae, q.4, a.8.

> On the part of its cause . . . a thing which has a more certain cause, is itself more certain. In this way faith is more certain than those three virtues, because it is founded on the Divine truth, whereas the aforesaid three virtues [wisdom, science and understanding] are based on human reason.[65]

When we accept as certain something that is not obvious, our attitude in faith is humble. Quite generally, we have to accept that others can know more than we do, and we trust such persons more than our own opinion:

> A man of little science is more certain about what he hears on the authority of an expert in science, than about what is apparent to him according to his own reason: and much more is a man certain about what he hears from God, Who cannot be deceived, than about what he sees with his own reason, which can be mistaken.[66]

If we do not recognize our faith to be certain, it simply becomes a human opinion among others, and divine Revelation becomes useless. Of course the certainty of faith does not mean, on the other hand, that a believer never asks questions to God, but that he knows on which basis he asks his questions.

In the ecumenical search for a criterion of discernment among different Christian traditions, the Catholic contribution is one of certainty. As Pope Paul VI said during Vatican II:

> If you have the understanding of this great problem of the recomposition of Christians into the unity wanted by Christ, if you have the perception of its importance and of its historical maturing, you will feel rising from the depth of your soul a wonderful and precise witnessing to that Catholic safety, which will tell you within yourself: I am already in the unity wanted by Christ; I am already within his flock, because I am Catholic, because I am with Peter.

---

65 Ibid.

66 *ST* ad 2.

> This is a great privilege, this is a great consolation; Catholics, enjoy it. Faithful, be conscious of that privileged position, due of course not to the merit of anybody, but to the goodness of God, who called us to such a happy position.[67]

In his encyclical on ecumenism, Pope John Paul II also said:

> The Catholic Church thus affirms that during the two thousand years of her history she has been preserved in unity, with all the means with which God wishes to endow his Church, and this despite the often grave crises which have shaken her, the infidelity of some of her ministers, and the faults into which her members daily fall. The Catholic Church knows that, by virtue of the strength which comes to her from the Spirit, the weaknesses, mediocrity, sins and at times the betrayals of some of her children cannot destroy what God has bestowed on her as part of his plan of grace. Moreover, "the powers of death shall not prevail against it" (Mt 16:18). Even so, the Catholic Church does not forget that many among her members cause God's plan to be discernible only with difficulty. Speaking of the lack of unity among Christians, the Decree on Ecumenism does not ignore the fact that "people of both sides were to blame," and acknowledges that responsibility cannot be attributed only to the "other side." By God's grace, however, neither what belongs to the structure of the Church of Christ nor that communion which still exists with the other Churches and Ecclesial Communities has been destroyed.[68]

Catholic theologians must deal with a paradox: all Christians are divided, but the Catholic Church alone has never lost full unity, and the fullness of the means of grace of the Church of Christ is in her alone. Do only the non-Catholics have to work for ecumenism, then? Or does ecumenical dialogue mean that the other Christians must go back to Catholic fullness and that the Catholic Church just

[67] Paul VI, General Audience, 22 January 1964, *Osservatore Romano,* Edizione quotidiane italiana, 23 January 1964, 1. (My translation.)

[68] John Paul II, Encyclical *Ut Unum Sint* (25 May 1995), §11.

invites them and waits? The fullness of the means of salvation—and therefore of unity—does not prevent the Catholic Church from a progress in perfection, because "this unity subsists in the Catholic Church as something she can never lose, and we hope that it will continue to increase until the end of time." [69] The root of Catholic ecumenism is not a recovery of a unity she would have lost—we always confess in the Creed that the Church is one—but an increased fidelity: "Every renewal of the Church is essentially grounded in an increase of fidelity to her own calling. Undoubtedly this is the basis of the movement toward unity." [70]

SUMMARY

What God reveals to us is infinitely superior to what we could find by ourselves. In order that people can believe, the content of faith must be announced to them, by persons whom God sends. This is the first condition for faith. Everybody knows that what is preached could be wrong, and the diversity of preaching makes it impossible not to notice such a problem. How can we know in the third millennium that what is preached to us really is Jesus Christ and his message? The theological school of St. Thomas Aquinas says that God, who does not want his revelation to be lost, gave the authority of the Church as a rule by which any preaching must be measured. Of course that authority is not only the one of the pope, as if the other bishops were not real bishops, and the ministry of the pope does not consist only in checking what is preached, but in case of crucial doubts the pope has the last word.

This question of authority is at the very center of ecumenical dialogue. The 1963 Assembly of Faith and Order in Montreal shows that Protestant theologians can and must overcome a certain doubt regarding "Tradition": the simple fact of meeting other

[69] Council Vatican II, Decree on Ecumenism, *Unitatis Redintegratio,* §4.
[70] Ibid., §6.

Christians shows that all live in a certain tradition, and in any case the Bible must always be interpreted. "Tradition" is the Gospel transmitted, but it is transmitted in different Christian traditions. How can we know whether one particular tradition is totally, partially, or not at all faithful to the Gospel? Montreal gives useful criteria of discernment: apostolic faith, correct interpretation of the Bible under the guidance of the Holy Spirit, reading of any biblical text in the light of the whole Scripture or of some basic principles, of the ancient Councils . . . but none of these criteria completely solves the problem of Christian diversity. Historical scholarship offers a great help, but cannot solve all points on obscure questions, and cannot substitute divine authority (required by faith). To declare previously divided Christians to be newly united would in any case require an authority clearly supported by God himself. The Catholic Church, conscious as she is of the many sins of her members, offers to ecumenism her firm certainty never to have lost faith, always to have kept the fullness of the means of salvation. Without such a certainty, the gift of divine revelation and Christian unity remains doubtful. Without the possibility of declaring faith with certainty, ecumenism could never declare previously divided Christians to be one, and an endless dialogue would become an end in itself.

CHAPTER FIVE

Second Condition for a Human Response: The Assent

THE SECOND CONDITION of faith is the assent given to the faith that has been preached. And this assent is possible only with grace. It is important to highlight this fact in order not to put the main weight on human actions, whether it be the human act of preaching or the human assent. Without divine action, it is simply meaningless to speak about faith. It is also necessary to see the connection between divine grace and human actions. How is the Church connected to divine grace?

GRACE AS A CONDITION FOR FAITH

Even if faith—which in any case must come from God—is rightly announced by human witnesses, it remains possible for the listener not to believe. For St. Thomas, one cannot believe unless he is helped by divine grace:

> As regards the second [condition for faith], viz. man's assent to the things which are of faith, we may observe a twofold cause, one of external inducement, such as seeing a miracle, or being persuaded by someone to embrace the faith: neither of which is a sufficient cause, since of those who see the same miracle, or who hear the same sermon, some believe, and some do not. Hence we must assert

> another internal cause, which moves man inwardly to assent to matters of faith. The Pelagians held that this cause was nothing else than man's free-will: and consequently they said that the beginning of faith is from ourselves, inasmuch as, to wit, it is in our power to be ready to assent to things which are of faith, but that the consummation of faith is from God, Who proposes to us the things we have to believe. But this is false, for, since man, by assenting to matters of faith, is raised above his nature, this must needs accrue to him from some supernatural principle moving him inwardly; and this is God. Therefore faith, as regards the assent which is the chief act of faith, is from God moving man inwardly by grace.[1]

The main reason grace is needed is not that the content of faith is difficult to understand. It is that we are raised above our nature by our participation in divine life. Then, in addition to this, the typical objects of faith are also above our capacity of understanding. For Aquinas, we cannot, for instance, discover that God is Trinity with our reason, and if we would try to prove the Trinity we would empty our faith and make it ridiculous.[2] We always need divine action so that we can think (or do anything else), but in the case of faith, divine grace pulls our thought above our natural capacities.[3] Finally, as I have already said, the fact that faith implies changing our life tends to make us reluctant to make the assent of faith.

To know God is the only possibility for us to be fully happy. God has freely decided not only to let us know him as well as human beings can, but to raise us up to the level of his divine life (by adoption). This requires divine grace. How does this happen?

---

[1] *ST* IIa IIae, q.6, a.1.

[2] Cf., e.g., ibid., Ia, q.32, a.1; *Super Boethii De Trinitate,* pars 1, q.1, a.4.

[3] Cf. *ST* Ia IIae, q.109, a.1: "We must say that for the knowledge of any truth whatsoever man needs Divine help, that the intellect may be moved by God to its act. But he does not need a new light added to his natural light, in order to know the truth in all things, but only in some that surpass his natural knowledge. And yet at times God miraculously instructs some by His grace in things that can be known by natural reason, even as He sometimes brings about miraculously what nature can do."

What is the human element in it, if there is any? Are we still free human beings? Do we take part in the grace-giving process?

Grace Helps Human Acceptance of the Divine Proposal

For St. Thomas Aquinas, we have free will because we are rational beings, and without free will the whole field of ethics would disappear.[4] The act of free will consists in a collaboration of knowledge and will (desire): we know different possibilities and we choose one of them that we consider to be good.[5]

Our choices depend on what we already know. Before we know anything no choice can be made, because the elements among which we might choose are not present to our mind. Some criteria of choice should also be present before the choice itself. Generally speaking, the human act of free will cannot be totally independent from God,[6] but when the object of a choice is totally above the capacities of human nature, divine help is more explicitly and radically indispensable:

> Nothing can act beyond its species, since the cause must always be more powerful than its effect. Now the gift of grace surpasses every capability of created nature, since it is nothing short of a partaking of the Divine Nature, which exceeds every other nature.

[4] Cf. *ST* Ia, q.83, a.1.

[5] Cf. *ST* Ia IIae, q.13, a.1.

[6] Cf. *ST* Ia IIae, q.109, a.2, ad 1: "Man is master of his acts and of his willing or not willing, because of his deliberate reason, which can be bent to one side or another. And although he is master of his deliberating or not deliberating, yet this can only be by a previous deliberation; and since it cannot go on to infinity, we must come at length to this, that man's free-will is moved by an extrinsic principle, which is above the human mind, to wit by God, as the Philosopher proves in the chapter 'On Good Fortune'. Hence the mind of man still unweakened is not so much master of its act that it does not need to be moved by God; and much more the free-will of man weakened by sin, whereby it is hindered from good by the corruption of the nature." Cf. also Ia IIae, q.13, a.6.

> And thus it is impossible that any creature should cause grace. For it is as necessary that God alone should deify, bestowing a partaking of the Divine Nature by a participated likeness as it is impossible that anything save fire should enkindle.[7]

We can decide to accept God's gift or not, but even the preparation for grace in our free will must come from God:

> If we speak of grace as it signifies a help from God to move us to good, no preparation is required on man's part, that, as it were, anticipates the Divine help, but rather, every preparation in man must be by the help of God moving the soul to good. And thus even the good movement of the free-will, whereby anyone is prepared for receiving the gift of grace is an act of the free-will moved by God. And thus man is said to prepare himself, according to Prov. 16:1: "It is the part of man to prepare the soul"; yet it is principally from God, Who moves the free-will.[8]

The act of free will in which we accept justification by God is really an act of our free will—because what is saved is a naturally free being—but this act is possible only with divine help. God himself acts so that we are able to act freely:

> God moves everything in its own manner. . . . Hence He moves man to justice according to the condition of his human nature. But it is man's proper nature to have free-will. Hence in him who has the use of reason, God's motion to justice does not take place without a movement of the free-will; but He so infuses the gift of justifying grace that at the same time He moves the free-will to accept the gift of grace, in such as are capable of being moved thus.[9]

First comes a divine act that grants us grace so that we can accept the divine offer. In ourselves, the acceptance by the free will is the

---

[7] *ST* Ia IIae, q.112, a.1. Cf. Ia IIae, q.109, a.5.
[8] *ST* Ia IIae, q.112, a.2.
[9] *ST* Ia IIae, q.113, a.3.

beginning of our union with God, granted that such a beginning is possible only thanks to a previous divine initiative.[10]

Is Divine Help an Obstacle to Human Freedom?

If the desire of any human heart can be fully satisfied only in God, and if that can happen only with divine grace, a question appears: Are we still real human beings? Are we still free? Is human fulfillment obtained at the price of our humanity? Such a highly sensitive question has received different answers throughout history.

The main Reformers denied the possibility of human freedom at God's expense. Martin Luther is especially clear on this point:

> Just as we do not come into being by our own will, but by necessity, so we do not do anything by right of free choice, but as God has foreknown and as he leads us to act by his infallible and immutable counsel and power.[11]

Luther did not consider this point to be at the margin of Christian life. He published a whole work against Erasmus on the question, and he took that great "political" risk because of the central importance it had in his system:

> Therefore, it is not irreverent, or superfluous, but essentially salutary and necessary for a Christian, to find out whether the will does anything or nothing in matters pertaining to eternal salvation. . . . If we do not know these things, we shall know nothing at all of things Christian, and we shall be worse than any heathen.[12]

---

[10] Cf. *ST* Ia IIae, q.8.

[11] Martin Luther, *The Bondage of the Will* (*De servo arbitrio*, 1525), vol. 33, *Luther's Works* (Philadelphia: Fortress Press, 1972), 191.

[12] Ibid., 35.

Within Luther's system, such a position is necessary, because he does not see how a human action could be at the same time a divine action. Many modern and contemporary thinkers will have the same difficulty, which basically leads to a choice between God and human beings: Luther denied human actions for the sake of God, modern atheists will feel obliged to deny God for the sake of the human being. Human freedom is at the heart of this question.

For St. Thomas Aquinas the whole question is not asked correctly if it leads to an opposition between divine and human action within human free acts. He insists on human freedom, although not understood as independence from God. We cannot choose the final end of all actions, which is an infinite happiness to be found only in God. But we can choose different means to reach that happiness. We can even make choices that are against that final end, because we do not see God and can identify our happiness with minor but more immediate goods:

> Man wills Happiness of necessity, nor can he will not to be happy, or to be unhappy. Now since choice is not of the end, but of the means . . . ; it is not of the perfect good, which is Happiness, but of other particular goods. Therefore man chooses not of necessity, but freely.[13]

The fact that we can use our free will against our final end—that is, against God—is not a proof of our freedom. It is just a sign of the weakness of our free will, acting against our deepest desire:

> We note a second difference regarding which there can be free choice as the difference between good and evil. But this difference does not intrinsically belong to the power of free choice but is incidentally related to the power inasmuch as natures capable of defect have such free choice. For inasmuch as the will of itself is ordained for good as its proper object, the will can strive for evil only insofar as evil is understood under the aspect of good, and

[13] *ST* Ia IIae, q.13, a.6.

> such understanding belongs to a deficiency of the intellect or reason, which causes choice to be free. But it does not belong to the nature of a power to be deficient in its activity. For example, it does not belong to the nature of the power of sight that one see things indistinctly.[14]

It is perfectly possible to keep our free will in a situation in which our choices are always good. In such a situation, free will is still acting:

> Although a creature would be better if it adhered unchangeably to God, nevertheless that one also is good which can adhere to God or not adhere. And so a universe in which both sorts of creatures are found is better than if only one or the other were found. . . . If however, any creature adheres unchangeably to God, it is not on this account deprived of free choice, because it can do or not do many things while adhering to God.[15]

Our free will is not lost—and becomes even stronger—when we choose the divine will. The saints in Heaven can choose to accept our prayers or not—which is an act of their free will—and of course God can choose to accept their prayers and ours: he is supremely free. Divine help does not prevent our free will from acting, quite the opposite: grace makes our acceptance of the divine will possible, without making it necessary, because God respects our nature:

[14] Thomas Aquinas, *De Malo,* q.16, a.5 [*The De Malo of Thomas Aquinas,* with facing-page translation by Richard Regan, Edited with an Introduction and Notes by Brian Davies (Oxford/New York: Oxford University Press, 2001)].

[15] Thomas Aquinas, *De Veritate,* q.24, a.1, ad 16 [St. Thomas Aquinas, *Truth,* vol. III, trans. Robert W. Schmidt (Chicago: Henry Regnery Company, 1954)]. Cf. *De Malo,* q.16, a.5: "And so nothing prevents there being a power of free choice that so strives for good that it is in no way capable of striving for evil, whether by nature, as in the case of God, or by the perfection of grace, as in the case of the saints and the holy angels."

> Every form inclines the subject after the mode of the subject's nature. Now it is the mode of an intellectual nature to be inclined freely towards the objects it desires. Consequently the movement of grace does not impose necessity; but he who has grace can fail to make use of it, and can sin.[16]

God's gift can be received only with God's help. It is possible to refuse it, and such a choice is the main point of our present life. Anyone who would refuse to be with God would in fact diminish his own humanity by restricting to finite goods the desire of a heart made for the infinite. If such an attitude is persistent, it can lead to hell, about which the *Catechism of the Catholic Church* says:

> The chief punishment of hell is eternal separation from God, in whom alone man can possess the life and happiness for which he was created and for which he longs.[17]

If, on the other hand, one chooses to be with God, this implies a submission. Is that against human dignity? Not only is it in fact impossible to live a human life without any kind of submission, but to be submitted to the highest being is our real dignity.[18]

DIVINE HELP CORRESPONDS TO HUMAN NATURE

If we do not refuse to depend upon God, we can open our life to our Creator. This is the condition for the fulfillment of our deepest desires of happiness. The Truth of Jesus Christ offers us true freedom, at different levels:

> The best [of the gifts] is that acquisition of freedom which knowledge of truth brings about in believers; this is why [Christ] says

[16] *ST* Ia, q.62, a.3, ad 2.

[17] *Catechism of the Catholic Church,* §1035.

[18] Cf. *ST* IIa IIae, q.81, a.7: "By the very fact that we revere and honor God, our mind is subjected to Him; wherein its perfection consists."

> *The truth will make you free* (Jn 8:32). Here, "to free" does not imply exemption from absolutely any kind of limitation . . . , it means strictly "to make free," and that from three things: the truth of doctrine will free us from the error of falsity: *My mouth will meditate on truth, and my lips will detest the impious* (Prov 8:7); the truth of grace will free us from the servitude of sin: *The law of the Spirit of life in Christ Jesus will free me from the law of sin and death* (Rom 8:2); the truth of eternity, in Christ Jesus, will free us from corruption: *the creature itself will be freed from the servitude of corruption* (Rom 8:21).[19]

This text is very realistic: we are not freed from any limitation or difficulty *(angustia)*. We are still limited beings (as all creatures are in any case) in a difficult world. But the Savior frees us from the mistakes at the doctrinal and moral levels: our happiness can thus become deeper already in this life and we can prepare ourselves for the vision of God. There, in heaven, the last liberation is the liberation from death. Wasn't that Plato's and Aristotle's desire?

That such a liberation is possible thanks only to God does not mean that it is not our liberation, since it corresponds to our nature:

> According to the Philosopher (Metaph. i, 2), what is "free is cause of itself." Therefore he acts freely, who acts of his own accord. Now man does of his own accord that which he does from a habit that is suitable to his nature: since a habit inclines one as a second nature. If, however, a habit be in opposition to nature, man would not act according to his nature, but according to some corruption affecting that nature. Since then the grace of the Holy Ghost is like an interior habit bestowed on us and inclining us to act aright, it makes us do freely those things that are becoming to grace, and shun what is opposed to it. Accordingly the New Law is called the law of liberty in two respects. First, because it does not bind us to do or avoid certain things, except such as are of

---

[19] Thomas Aquinas, *Commentary on John* 8:32 (1199). (My translation. I thank Fr. Simon Tugwell, O.P. for his help.)

> themselves necessary or opposed to salvation, and come under the prescription or prohibition of the law. Secondly, because it also makes us comply freely with these precepts and prohibitions, inasmuch as we do so through the promptings of grace. It is for these two reasons that the New Law is called "the law of perfect liberty" (James 1:25).[20]

Not only does divine help not prevent us from being ourselves, but it makes it possible for us to be what we should be—according to our nature—but could not be if left solely to our own capacities. This help really makes us free, and respects our freedom: Christians receive some basic rules of life and determine, with the help of the Spirit in their heart and with their reason, how to apply these basic principles to concrete situations.

On top of that, divine help is granted also through human means.

HUMAN MEANS OF GRACE

As it has already been said about the authorship of the Bible, God uses human means. He uses them even in the granting of his grace. First of all, Jesus' humanity is an instrument of his divinity, although this must be understood accurately: his humanity is not an external instrument like a hammer in our hand, but an instrument united to the Person of the Word;[21] this is strictly unique. Therefore, he is not a passive instrument (like a hammer), but an instrument according to his active human nature:

> It is proper to an instrument to be moved by the principal agent, yet diversely, according to the property of its nature. For an inanimate instrument, as an axe or a saw, is moved by the craftsman with only a corporeal movement; but an instrument animated by a sensitive soul is moved by the sensitive appetite, as a horse by its

[20] *ST* Ia IIae, q.108, a.1, ad 2.
[21] Cf. *ST* IIIa, q.2, a.6, ad 4.

rider; and an instrument animated with a rational soul is moved by its will, as by the command of his lord the servant is moved to act, the servant being like an animate instrument, as the Philosopher says. And hence it was in this manner that the human nature of Christ was the instrument of the Godhead, and was moved by its own will.[22]

Then, as we have seen regarding biblical authorship, an action of the divinity and of the human instrument is the same unique action, although each cause acts at a different level:

> The instrument is said to act through being moved by the principal agent; and yet, besides this, it can have its proper operation through its own form, as stated above of fire. And hence the action of the instrument as instrument is not distinct from the action of the principal agent; yet it may have another operation, inasmuch as it is a thing. Hence the operation of Christ's human nature, as the instrument of the Godhead, is not distinct from the operation of the Godhead; for the salvation wherewith the manhood of Christ saves us and that wherewith His Godhead saves us are not distinct; nevertheless, the human nature in Christ, inasmuch as it is a certain nature, has a proper operation distinct from the Divine.[23]

We see in the Gospels that Jesus uses his body to heal, and similarly—says Aquinas—his humanity is an instrument of our own resurrection.[24] Of course Jesus' humanity can so work only because it is united to his divinity:

> An instrument does not bring forth the action of the principal agent by its own power, but in virtue of the principal agent. Hence Christ's humanity does not cause grace by its own power,

---

[22] *ST* IIIa, q.18, a.1, ad 2.
[23] *ST* IIIa, q.19, a.1, ad 2.
[24] Cf. Thomas Aquinas, *Commentary of the Sentences,* Book IV, d.43, q. unica, a.2, q.1.

> but by virtue of the Divine Nature joined to it, whereby the actions of Christ's humanity are saving actions.[25]

If God can use humanity in the specific case of the Son incarnate, he can also use other human instruments, in a way partly similar and partly (mainly) different, because:

> Christ had the fulness, since inasmuch as His soul was united to the Godhead, He had the perfect power of effecting all these acts [miracles]. But other saints who are moved by God as separated and not united instruments, receive power in a particular manner in order to bring about this or that act.[26]

Similarly, the sacraments are created instruments of God:

> As in the person of Christ the humanity causes our salvation by grace, the Divine power being the principal agent, so likewise in the sacraments of the New Law, which are derived from Christ, grace is instrumentally caused by the sacraments, and principally by the power of the Holy Ghost working in the sacraments, according to Jn. 3:5: "Unless a man be born again of water and the Holy Ghost he cannot enter into the kingdom of God."[27]

In the sacraments, grace is given through inanimate created realities (e.g. bread, wine, water), and also thanks to rational created realities: e.g. the human minister and the person who receives the sacrament. Thomas summarizes in a very clear and synthetic text the relationship between Jesus as instrument and other created instruments of grace which depend upon him:[28]

---

[25] *ST* Ia IIae, q.112, a.1, ad 1.

[26] *ST* IIIa, q.7, a.7, ad 1.

[27] *ST* Ia IIae, q.112, a.1, ad 2.

[28] Christ has what Thomas calls the "power of excellence" in the sacraments. (They come from his Passion and his institution and he can bestow their effect without the sacrament, cf. *ST* IIIa, q.64, a.3.) This belongs only to him, cf. IIIa, q.64, a.4, ad 3: "It was in order to avoid the

Since Christ intended to withdraw His bodily presence from the Church, He needed to institute other men as ministers to Himself, who should dispense the Sacraments to the faithful. Hence He committed to His disciples the consecration of His Body and Blood, saying: *Do this in memory of me* (Luke xxii, 19). He gave them the power of forgiving sins, according to the text: *Whose sins you shall forgive, they are forgiven them* (John xx, 23). He enjoined on them the function of baptising: *Go, teach all nations, baptising them* (Matt xxviii, 19). Now a minister stands to his master as an instrument to a prime agent. An instrument must be proportionate to the agent: therefore the ministers of Christ must be conformable to Him. But Christ, our Lord and Master, by His own power and might worked out our salvation, inasmuch as He was both God and man. As man, He suffered for our redemption; as He was God, His suffering brought salvation to us. The ministers of Christ then must be men, and at the same time have some share in the Divinity *(aliquid divinitatis participare)* in point of spiritual power: for an instrument too has some share in the power of the prime agent. Nor can it be said that this power was given to the disciples of Christ not to be transmitted to others. It was *given unto edification* (2 Cor. xiii, 10), to the building up of the Church, and must be perpetuated so long as the Church needs building up, that is, *to the end of the world* (Matt xxviii, 20). And since spiritual effects are transmitted to us from Christ under sensible signs, this power had to be delivered to men under some such signs—certain forms of words, definite acts, as imposition of hands, anointing, the delivery of a book or chalice, and the like. Whenever anything spiritual is delivered under a corporeal sign, that is called a Sacrament. Thus in the conferring of spiritual power a Sacrament is wrought, which is called the Sacrament of Order. Now it is a point of divine liberality that the bestowal of power should be accompanied with the means of duly exercising that power. But the spiritual power of administering the

---

incongruity of many heads in the Church, that Christ was unwilling to communicate to ministers His power of excellence. If, however, He had done so, He would have been Head in chief; the others in subjection to Him."

> Sacraments requires divine grace for its convenient exercise: therefore in this Sacrament, as in other Sacraments, grace is bestowed. Among Sacraments the noblest, and that which sets the crown on the rest, is the Sacrament of the Eucharist. Therefore the power of Order must be considered chiefly in relation to this Sacrament: for everything is ruled by the end for which it is made. Now the power that gives perfection, also prepares the matter to receive it. Since, then, the power of Order extends to the consecration of the Body of Christ and the administration of the same to the faithful, it must further extend to the rendering of the faithful fit and worthy for the reception of that Sacrament. But the believer is rendered fit and worthy by being free from sin: otherwise he cannot be united with Christ spiritually, with whom he is sacramentally united in the reception of this Sacrament. The power of Order therefore must extend to the remission of sins by the administration of those Sacraments which are directed to that purpose, Baptism and Penance.[29]

In the case of grace as in the case of announcing the faith, God can use created and, above all, human instruments. This is due, as I have already said, not to our own native capacities, of course, but to the goodness of God who "has wished to communicate His likeness to creatures, not only in point of their being, but likewise in point of their being causes of other things." [30] The fact that God acts through created instruments appears in the very first place in the Incarnation of his Son, which aims at helping us according to our nature.[31] Depending upon that main and central event, other means of grace are used. The next chapter will present the Church as a means of grace.

---

[29] Thomas Aquinas, *Summa contra Gentiles,* Book IV, chap. 74.

[30] Ibid., Book III, chap. 70.

[31] Cf. *ST* IIa IIae, q.83, a.3, ad 2: "Such is the weakness of the human mind that it needs a guiding hand, not only to the knowledge, but also to the love of Divine things by means of certain sensible objects known to us. Chief among these is the humanity of Christ, according to the words of the Preface, 'that through knowing God visibly, we may be caught up to the love of things invisible.' "

Summary

After Chapter Four, which dealt with the Church's preaching as one condition for faith, Chapter Five speaks about grace as another condition for faith. Faith must be preached and grace given to anybody who may decide to believe, or not to believe.

Faith is about mysteries far above our human capacity of understanding. We are called to share divine life. Faith requires that we change some aspects of our life. For all these reasons, no faith is possible without divine grace. Still, to accept faith is a fully human act, prepared and made possible by grace but nonetheless human. We can decide to use divine help or to refuse it. Without grace, we could not accept the divine invitation to eternal life, nor could we even refuse it in a well-informed way.

To be helped by God is not opposed to our human freedom. Without God, our freedom as well as we ourselves would simply not exist. But God precisely makes our freedom possible and wants it. We can refuse his help: such a refusal would be a sign of our free will, but also a sign of its weakness. Real freedom implies following our human nature, which implies a desire for God. Being out of step with our human nature, we would not really be free because we would not fully be ourselves.

Without faith there is no Church. Without grace there is no faith. Therefore without grace there is no Church. But the relationship between grace and the Church is broader than this aspect. God chooses to use created elements not only as recipients of grace, but also as instruments of grace: Jesus' humanity first, and then, depending upon that, human beings and sacraments. Human beings are means of grace for themselves (when they decide to accept grace) and for others, especially in sacramental ministry. The next chapter will develop the relationship between the Church and grace: the Church is not only the recipient and means for the transmission of grace. The Church can be understood in her deepest identity only as "the place of grace."

CHAPTER SIX

The Church as a Place of Grace

AS WE HAVE already seen, for Aquinas, Christ is "the head of all human beings in regard to grace."[1] Such a view of the Church is in sharp contrast with the so-called "Bellarminian" understanding, which has led to the common "sociological" meaning of the word "Church" in contemporary society. St. Thomas's identification of Church and "realm of grace" provides a solid framework for the understanding of the relationship between the Catholic Church and other Christians, as well as between Christianity and other religions.

"BELLARMINIAN" ECCLESIOLOGY

St. Robert Bellarmine (1542–1621), Doctor of the Church, was a leading figure of the Catholic Counter-Reformation. In order to react against what he perceived as a Protestant (mainly Calvinist) insistence on the invisible aspect of the Church and a parallel underestimation of her visible aspect, he tried to coin a minimal definition of the Church.[2] His main purpose was to provide a way of recognizing who does belong to the Church and who does not:

[1] *ST* IIIa, q.19, a.4, ad 1.

[2] Contemporary research and dialogue have led to a more precise understanding of the reasons why the Reformers insisted on the invisible aspect of the Church, and of the remaining role the visible aspect had for them.

There are three parts of the definition, namely: Profession of the true faith, Communion of Sacraments, and Subjection to the Roman Pontiff, the legitimate Pastor. By reason of the first part are excluded all unbelievers, as well those who were never in the Church, like the Jews, Pagans and Turks, as those who were formerly in the Church but have left it, like heretics and apostates. By reason of the second part are excluded Catechumens and those who are excommunicated; the first because they have not been admitted to a participation of the Sacraments, the second because they have been debarred from them. By reason of the third part are excluded Schismatics, who have the Faith and the Sacraments, but are not subject to the legitimate Pastor; and therefore, they profess the Faith and receive the Sacraments outside (the true Church). All other people, even when they are wicked and abandoned criminals, are included. The difference between our definition and all others is that all the rest require internal virtues to constitute a person in the Church, and, therefore, they make the true Church something invisible. Whereas they also believe that in the Church are found all the virtues: faith, hope and charity, and all the rest. However, for anyone to be called in some sense a part of the true Church, of which the Scriptures speak, we do not think that any internal virtue is required, but only an external profession of faith and communication of the Sacraments, which can be perceived by the senses themselves. For the Church is an assembly of men, as visible and palpable as the assembly of the Roman people, or the Kindgom of France, or the Republic of the Venetians. The internal gifts of the Holy Spirit: faith, hope, and charity, and the rest are the soul. The external profession of faith and communication of the Sacraments are the body. From which it follows that some people belong to both the soul and the body of the Church, and are, therefore, united to Christ, the Head, both interiorly and exteriorly. And these are most perfectly in the Church. They are like living members in the body, although among them, too, some participate more and some less in the life, and some have only the beginnings of life, hav-

My purpose here is not to enter that debate, but to explain Bellarmine's motivation.

> ing, as it were, sensation without movement, like those who have faith without charity. Others, however, are of the soul but not of the body, as Catechumens and those who have been excommunicated, who may have faith and charity, which is possible. Finally, some belong to the body and not to the soul (of the Church), like those who have no internal virtue, but yet, out of the hope or (moved) by some temporal fear, they profess the faith and share in the Sacraments, under the rule of legitimate pastors. Our definition comprehends only this last mode of being in the Church . . . the minimum required for anyone to be called a part of the visible Church.[3]

It seems that the Church can be understood without any consideration of spiritual elements: it is mainly a sociological body, easily identified. We can see here how a polemical context leads people to reduce their own point of view. Of course St. Robert Bellarmine was a spiritual man, who never thought of denying the importance of the spiritual life, but his working definition of the Church was received independently of his personal spiritual attitude and of his more complete thought. It is not difficult to see how such a reduced ecclesiology persists in the contemporary mindset: The baptized Catholics (above all the clergy) are "The Catholic Church," no matter how holy or sinful they might be, and non-Catholics are something else. I will soon mention some consequences of this mindset. The contrast to St. Thomas who considered all human beings of all times to be members of the Church, although in different ways, is obvious. Doesn't Bellarmine himself say that his definition is different from all others?

To speak about the body and the soul of the Church does not necessarily imply a Bellarminian ecclesiology, and to refuse to apply body and soul to the Church does not necessarily mean to move

[3] St. Robert Bellarmine, *De controversiis christianae fidei adversus hujus temporis haereticos,* II, lib.3, *De Ecclesia militante,* caput II, translation in John A. Hardon, *A Comparative Study of Bellarmine's Doctrine of the Relation of Sincere Non-Catholics to the Catholic Church* (Rome: Excerpta ex dissertatione. . . , Pontificia Universitas Gregoriana, 1951), 15–17, 21–23.

away from Bellarminian ecclesiology. Bellarmine opposed Calvinist ecclesiology (as he perceived it), but depended on some of the presuppositions of what he rejected. One should reject the weak aspects of Bellarminian ecclesiology without assuming its perhaps unconscious presuppositions. This is why I shall try to find a solution that would be prior to the Reformation–Counter-Reformation, and that may help solve contemporary questions.

The next section will try to go back to a pre-Bellarminian view of body and soul of the Church. An ecclesiology that insists on the Body of Christ seems to me to be the best way of avoiding the problems that arise from a sociological ecclesiology. Of course the Church must be understood as the People of God,[4] *congregatio fidelium*[5] (congregation of the faithful), or "Holy City,"[6] but such expressions are more open to a Bellarminian understanding (although it is not the only possible understanding). Of course "Body of Christ" or "Bride of Christ"[7] could also be understood sociologically, but I think that such views of the Church—rooted in their patristic and medieval meaning—are especially apt to correct sociological misunderstandings.

GRACE AND THE BODY OF THE CHURCH AS "COEXTENSIVE"

Vatican II explicitly avoids a division between visible and "spiritual" elements of the Church, thus correcting the way Bellarmine's definition had been received throughout the centuries:

> The society structured with hierarchical organs and the Mystical Body of Christ are not to be considered as two realities, nor are

[4] Cf. *Lumen Gentium,* §§9–17.

[5] Cf. Thomas Aquinas, *Compendium theologiae,* Book I, chap.147.

[6] Cf. *Lumen Gentium,* §6; cf. also Thomas Aquinas, *Commentary on the Psalms,* on Psalm 45, n.3: "Haec civitas est Ecclesia. Psal. 86: *gloriosa dicta sunt de te, civitas Dei* et cetera."

[7] Cf. *Lumen Gentium,* §6; *Commentary on the Psalms,* on Psalm 44, n.7.

the visible assembly and the spiritual community, nor the earthly Church and the Church enriched with heavenly things; rather they form one complex reality which coalesces from a divine and a human element.[8]

In contrast with a mainly sociological understanding of the Church, the understanding set forth by Vatican II combines visible and invisible elements. In this section of Chapter Six, I will try to show how such a combination of visible and invisible can work. I suggest that behind different ecclesiological tendencies, there are different anthropologies, that is, different conceptions of what a human being is, or at least different ways of combining ecclesiology and anthropology.

Are human beings purely material? Our capacity of knowing and remembering objects that are not present (our experience of love and freedom) suggests that there is a certain immaterial dimension in us. Classical philosophy treats that dimension in terms of the "soul." The relationship between body and soul has been understood in different ways. In the school of Plato (ca. 428–347 B.C.) "the soul is the person,"[9] our body prevents real knowledge, and only death will free us and open up the possibility of pure knowledge.[10] For Aristotle (384–22 B.C.), our knowledge begins with sensitive knowledge, and

---

[8] *Lumen Gentium,* §8.

[9] Plato, *Alcibiades,* 130c.

[10] Cf. Plato, *Phaedo,* trans. Benjamin Jewett, 66b67b: "And when they consider all this, must not true philosophers make a reflection, of which they will speak to one another in such words as these: We have found, they will say, a path of speculation which seems to bring us and the argument to the conclusion that while we are in the body, and while the soul is mingled with this mass of evil, our desire will not be satisfied, and our desire is of the truth. For the body is a source of endless trouble to us by reason of the mere requirement of food. . . . Moreover, if there is time and an inclination toward philosophy, yet the body introduces a turmoil and confusion and fear into the course of speculation, and hinders us from seeing the truth: and all experience shows that if we would have pure knowledge of anything we must be quit of the body, and the soul in herself

the soul is what gives unity to our body.[11] Thomas Aquinas will follow an Aristotelian line on this question. For him, our body is not some kind of prison of the soul, but "it belongs to the very essence of the soul to be united to a body." [12] Even though our soul is immortal and therefore does not die with the body, nevertheless "the human soul, remaining in its own existence after separation from the body, has a natural aptitude and a natural tendency to embodiment." [13] He insists on the unity of the human person:

> Body and soul are not two actually existing substances; rather, the two of them together constitute one actually existing substance. For man's body is not actually the same while the soul is present and when it is absent; but the soul makes it to be actually.[14]

On this question, Thomas is original. His contemporary St. Bonaventure (1217–74), more influenced by Platonism, holds that

---

must behold all things in themselves: then I suppose that we shall attain that which we desire, and of which we say that we are lovers, and that is wisdom, not while we live, but after death, as the argument shows; for if while in company with the body the soul cannot have pure knowledge, one of two things seems to follow—either knowledge is not to be attained at all, or, if at all, after death. For then, and not till then, the soul will be in herself alone and without the body. In this present life, I reckon that we make the nearest approach to knowledge when we have the least possible concern or interest in the body, and are not saturated with the bodily nature, but remain pure until the hour when God himself is pleased to release us. And then the foolishness of the body will be cleared away and we shall be pure and hold converse with other pure souls, and know of ourselves the clear light everywhere; and this is surely the light of truth. For no impure thing is allowed to approach the pure. These are the sort of words, Simmias, which the true lovers of wisdom cannot help saying to one another, and thinking."

11 Cf. Aristotle, *De Anima,* 412a 20: "The soul must be a substance in the sense of the form of a natural body having life potentially within it."

12 *ST* Ia, q.76, a.1, ad 6.

13 Ibid.

14 *Summa contra Gentiles,* Book II, chap. 69.

human beings are composed of two substances[15]—body and soul—but avoids a negative view of the body by saying that the soul loves the body.[16] Nevertheless, Thomas's view on the question would become the common teaching of the Church:

> The unity of soul and body is so profound that one has to consider the soul to be the "form" of the body (Cf. Council of Vienne [1312]: DS 902): i.e., it is because of its spiritual soul that the body made of matter becomes a living, human body; spirit and matter, in man, are not two natures united, but rather their union forms a single nature.[17]

Different anthropologies lead to different ecclesiologies. When Bellarmine considers it possible that some belong to the soul of the Church only, or to the body only, he presupposes an anthropology of two substances, or at least such an anthropology would be more coherent with his ecclesiology. Although the purpose of Bellarmine's system is to fight against Protestant ecclesiology, his understanding about a possible separation of body and soul is shared by Protestant theologians such as the French reformed pastor Pierre Jurieu (1637–1713):

> Body and soul must be united. Faith and charity must be together with the profession of faith, and the essence of the Church properly consists in both these things, and in their union. . . . [In the same way] one may not say that the body without the soul is a man. . . .

---

[15] Cf. Bonaventura, *Breviloquium,* Pars II, cap. X, ed. Quaracchi, t.V, 228: "Ut igitur in homine manifestaretur Dei potentia, ideo fecit eum ex naturis maxime distantibus, coniunctis in unam personam et naturam; cuiusmodi sunt corpus et anima, quorum unum est substantia corporea, alterum vero, scilicet anima, est substantia spiritualis et incorporea; quae in genere substantiae maxime distant."

[16] Cf. Bonaventura, *In Joan.* XV, 20; ed. Quaracchi, t.VI, 450: "magna est dilectio, qua mater diligit filium. . . . Maior, qua uxor virum. . . . Maxima animae ad corpus. . . ."

[17] *Catechism of the Catholic Church* (11 October 1992), §365.

> To belong to the human body, it is not necessary to take part in the soul and its influences; a dead arm is still an arm. I admit that it is not a perfect arm, because it does not take part in life. . . . Similarly, it is not necessary to take part in the body in order to belong to the soul: reason is a faculty of the soul which is independent from the body, because the soul still has reason when it is separated from the body. It is the same with regards to the body and the soul of the Church. In order to belong to the Church, properly speaking, one must have faith and the profession of faith. But in order to belong to the soul of the Church alone, it is not necessary to take part in her body, that is to say in what is visible.[18]

To apply to the Church the analogy of body and soul leads both Bellarmine and an important Protestant theologian of the same period to a kind of ecclesiological dualism. Some texts of the recent Magisterium could give the same impression. For instance, Vatican II says:

> This is the one Church of Christ which in the Creed is professed as one, holy, catholic and apostolic, which our Savior, after His Resurrection, commissioned Peter to shepherd, and him and the other apostles to extend and direct with authority, which He erected for all ages as "the pillar and mainstay of the truth." This Church constituted and organized in the world as a society, subsists in the Catholic Church, which is governed by the successor of Peter and by the Bishops in communion with him, although many elements of sanctification and of truth are found outside of its visible structure *[extra eius compaginem]*. These elements, as gifts belonging to the Church of Christ, are forces impelling toward catholic unity.[19]

---

[18] Pierre Jurieu, *Le vrai système de l'Église et la véritable Analyse de la foi. Où sont dissipées toutes les illusions que les controversistes Modernes, Prétendus Catholiques, ont voulu faire au public sur la Nature de l'Église, son Infaillibilité et le Juge des Controverses* (Dordrecht: Chez la Veuve de Caspar et chez Théodore Goris, 1686), L.I, ch. I, 11–13. (My translation.)

[19] *Lumen Gentium*, §8.

Such a text can be understood in different ways. Obviously, the Catholic Church recognizes that some people are baptized and sometimes also receive the Eucharist, or even are bishops, without being Catholic. Such persons belong to the Church, but are not in her full communion. Strictly speaking then, they are not out of the Church, if "Church" is not understood in a Bellarminian sense. The elements of partial communion have in themselves a tendency toward full communion.

Cardinal Charles Journet (1891–1975), who was a disciple of St. Thomas, developed a theology of the Church. Fr. Yves Congar (1904–95) said that Journet's ecclesiological synthesis was an implementation of St. Thomas' thought.[20] Actually, even though he did not develop explicitly the link between anthropology and ecclesiology, Journet insisted on the distinction between soul and body of the Church, without considering them like two substances. For him, the Church has two souls, one depending on the other: the Holy Spirit and the effect of his action in us, summarized in the highest effect of grace, namely charity:

> If the Trinity desires to live in the midst of creatures, if the Holy Spirit wants to become the principle, more than that—the host and the uncreated soul of the Church, her uncreated Soul, He will have to give to human beings some spiritual gifts to prepare them for destinies so high. These gifts will be like an outpouring of the capital grace present in the holy soul of Christ, Head of the Church, namely of his priestly power, of his grace, of his truth, which will become the elements, either presupposed, or constitutive, of the created soul of the Church; they are . . . the sacramental characters, the sacramental graces, and finally the right jurisdictional orientation as emanating from the jurisdictional powers and as received in the heart of the faithful. In short, to summarize everything with one

[20] Cf. Yves M.-J. Congar, O.P., *Esquisses du mystère de l'Église* (Paris: Cerf, 1953), 7: "This theology, in spite of some difficulty of vocabulary . . . appears as the application [to the Church] of St. Thomas' synthesis." (My translation.)

> word, it will be necessary that the Holy Spirit fill human beings with charity which is sacramental and "directed." This is, indeed, the created, undivided soul of the Church. This soul goes down towards human beings. It becomes incarnate in them. It transforms them internally. The permanent virtues and the secret capacities that it confers to them will be for them the principle of a new manner of acting, of working. Consequently, a change will occur in their external behaviors. The whole of these external demonstrations is the body of the Church.[21]

Journet insists on what he calls the "coextensivity"[22] of the body and the soul of the Church, namely:

> Where the created soul of the Church is, there is also her body; vice versa, where the body of the Church is, there is her soul.[23]

As is the case in us, the soul takes some "matter," gives life to it, and unifies it so that it is our body. The soul of the Church cannot be actively present without making the body:

> It is impossible, either that the soul of the Church, as received in men . . . does not work to reveal externally the body of the Church, or that the body of the Church can appear where her soul is not.[24]

Journet explicitly holds that a parallel exists between the Church and the human being or the Incarnation of the Son of God:

> The spirituality and visibility of the Church are no more opposed to one another than the soul and body of a human being or, better, than the divinity and humanity in Christ.[25]

---

21 Charles Journet, *L'Église du Verbe Incarné,* vol. 3 (Saint-Maurice: Saint-Augustin, 2000), 1434. (My translation.)

22 Neologism created by him.

23 Journet, *L'Église du Verbe Incarné,* vol. 2 (Saint-Maurice: Saint-Augustin, 1999), 43. (My translation.)

24 Journet, *L'Église du Verbe Incarné,* vol. 3, 1553. (My translation.)

25 Charles Journet, *The Theology of the Church* (San Francisco: Ignatius Press, 2004), 13.

We will have to see the practical implications of this principle of "coextensivity." At the "theoretical" level, the main point is that the understanding of the relationship between soul and body applies both to human beings and to the Church. Whoever thinks it possible to belong only to the body or only to the soul of the Church presupposes a "dualistic" anthropology, different from St. Thomas's anthropology. Thomas's disciples tend to prefer a more "psychosomatic" ecclesiology, like Journet's. And there is a deep reason for that parallel: God relates to us in the Church, and he relates to us according to what we are. According to an axiom of St. Thomas: "It belongs to Divine providence to provide for each one according as its condition requires." [26] A dualistic structure of the place where God relates to human beings—whose structure in turn is not dualistic—would be an odd choice, coming from our Creator.

Church Membership and Salvation

The relationship between the body and the soul of the Church has an immediate impact on the understanding of salvation. The question is this: Is it necessary to belong to the Church in order to be saved? There is a continuity and an evolution in the answer to such a question, which is a very sensitive one in our pluralistic world.

The basic traditional premise to any consideration of the link between Church and salvation is the strict connection between Christ and his Body—the Church. This link is clear and central to the Fathers of the Church and medieval theologians. What they want to express is what is said by or about Jesus Christ himself in the New Testament:

[26] *ST* IIIa, q.61, a.1. Cf. some texts already quoted: "God moves everything in its own manner. . . . Hence He moves man to justice according to the condition of his human nature" (*ST* Ia IIae, q.113, a.3); "It is proper to an instrument to be moved by the principal agent, yet diversely, according to the property of its nature" (*ST* IIIa, q.18, a.1, ad 2).

> I tell you the truth, the man who does not enter the sheep pen by the gate, but climbs in by some other way, is a thief and a robber. The man who enters by the gate is the shepherd of his sheep.[27]
>
> He is the stone you builders rejected, which has become the capstone. Salvation is found in no one else, for there is no other name under heaven given to men by which we must be saved.[28]

The conclusion of the Fathers of the Church is that since the Church is constituted by Christ's salvation as his Body, there cannot be any salvation outside the Church. St. Cyprian of Carthage (d. 258) seems to be the first to say explicitly, "There is no salvation outside the Church"[29] ("salus extra Ecclesiam non est") or "there can be no salvation for anyone except in the Church."[30] Other Church Fathers follow and develop a similar line of thought (although their views differ from Cyprian's about the conditions for a valid baptism).[31] The medieval Magisterium seems to hold a very firm interpretation of this theology:

> We are obliged by our faith to believe and to hold that there is one holy Catholic and apostolic church; indeed, we firmly believe and sincerely confess this, and that outside of this church there is neither salvation nor the remission of sins. . . . Moreover, we declare, state and define that for every human creature it is a matter of strict necessity for salvation to be subject to the Roman Pontiff.[32]

---

[27] John 10:1–2.

[28] Acts 4:11–12.

[29] Letter 73.21, St. Cyprian, *Letters* (1–81), trans. Sr. Rose Bernard Donna, C.S.J., *The Fathers of the Church* (Washington, DC: The Catholic University of America Press, 1964), 282.

[30] St Cyprian, *Letters* (1–81), Letter 4.4, 13. Original Epistula Epist. 4.IV, CCSL III.B, 24: "Nemini salus esse nisi in Ecclesia possit."

[31] For a summary of patristic thought on the question, cf. Francis A. Sullivan, *Salvation Outside the Church? Tracing the History of the Catholic Response* (London: Geoffrey Chapman, 1992), 14–43.

[32] Pope Boniface VIII, Bull *Unam Sanctam* (1302); Denzinger, 870 and 875; *The Christian Faith,* 804.

> [The holy Roman Church] firmly believes, professes and preaches that "no one remaining outside the Catholic Church, not only pagans," but also Jews, heretics or schismatics, can become partakers of eternal life; but they will go to the "eternal fire prepared for the devil and his angels" [Mt 25:41], unless before the end of their life they are joined to *(aggregati)* it. For union with the body of the Church is of so great importance that the sacraments of the Church are helpful to salvation only for those remaining in it; and fasts, almsgiving, other works of piety, and the exercises of a militant Christian life bear eternal rewards for them alone. "And no one can be saved, no matter how many alms one has given, even if shedding one's blood for the name of Christ, unless one remains in the bosom and unity of the Catholic Church."[33]

This teaching is quite radical, and we shall see that the Magisterium will interpret it in a milder way. Medieval theology already contains some principles that help add some nuances to what seems to be an extreme view. In this regard, the main "attenuating" principle, which is very central for the whole of moral theology, is that an act can be considered human only when arising out of a conscious decision:

> Of actions done by man those alone are properly called "human," which are proper to man as man. Now man differs from irrational animals in this, that he is master of his actions. Wherefore those actions alone are properly called human, of which man is master. Now man is master of his actions through his reason and will; whence, too, the free-will is defined as "the faculty and will of reason." Therefore those actions are properly called human which proceed from a deliberate will. And if any other actions are found in man, they can be called actions "of a man," but not properly "human" actions, since they are not proper to man as man. Now it is clear that whatever actions proceed from a power, are caused by that power in accordance with the nature of its object. But the

33 Council of Florence, *Decree for the Copts* (1442); Denzinger, 1351, *The Christian Faith,* 810.

> object of the will is the end and the good. Therefore all human actions must be for an end.[34]

Because human actions proceed from a "deliberate will," the gravity of a sin is judged not only according to the act itself, but also according to the consciousness of the sinner. For example, St. Thomas considers even the sin of idolatry (i.e., the act of worshipping creatures instead of God) as attenuated in the case of ignorance:

> The gravity of a sin may be considered in two ways. First, on the part of the sin itself, and thus idolatry is a most grievous sin. . . . Secondly, the gravity of a sin may be considered on the part of the sinner. Thus the sin of one that sins knowingly is said to be graver than the sin of one that sins through ignorance.[35]

On the basis of this general moral principle, no unconscious action can be said to be a sin, because strictly speaking it is not a human act. This is why, for example, there are different juridical categories of homicide. That also applies to Church membership, as Pope Pius IX (pope from 1846 to 1878) clearly states:

> And here, beloved Sons and venerable Brethren, it is necessary once more to mention and censure the serious error into which some Catholics have unfortunately fallen. For they are of the opinion that those who live in errors, estranged from the true faith and Catholic unity, can attain eternal life. This is in direct opposition to Catholic teaching. We all know that those who suffer from invincible ignorance with regard to our holy religion, if they carefully keep the precepts of the natural law which have been written by God in the hearts of all persons, if they are prepared to obey God, and if they lead a virtuous and dutiful life, can, by the power of divine light and grace, attain eternal life. For God, who knows completely the minds and souls, the thoughts and habits of all persons, will not permit, in

---

[34] *ST* Ia IIae, q.1, a.1.

[35] *ST* IIa IIae, q.94, a.3.

> accord with his infinite goodness and mercy, anyone who is not guilty of a voluntary fault to suffer eternal punishment. However, also well known is the Catholic dogma that no one can be saved outside the Catholic Church, and that those who obstinately oppose the authority of the definitions of the Church, and who stubbornly remain separated from the unity of the Church and from the successor of Peter the Roman Pontiff, to whom the Savior has entrusted the care of his vineyard, cannot obtain salvation.[36]

Pius IX maintains the traditional principle: no salvation outside the Church. But he adds a very basic moral principle: None are guilty of an ignorance that cannot be overcome. In a 1949 letter to the archbishop of Boston, the Holy Office condemned the opinion of Fr. Leonard Feeney, who held the strictest view of "outside the Church no salvation." The letter of the Holy Office first repeats the principle:

> The infallible dictum which teaches us that outside the Church there is no salvation is among the truths that the Church has always taught and will always teach. But this dogma is to be understood as the Church itself understands it. For the Savior did not leave it to private judgment to explain what is contained in the deposit of faith, but to the doctrinal authority of the Church.[37]

The letter then adds an interpretation of the principle. It insists on the fact that one who is in a situation of invincible ignorance can be saved by an implicit desire:

> As regards the helps to salvation which are ordered to the last end only by divine decree, not by intrinsic necessity, God, in his infinite

[36] Pius IX, Encyclical *Quanto Conficiamur Moerore* (10 August 1863); Denzinger 2865–67; *The Christian Faith,* 814. The same pope had said the same in some previous texts of minor authority, such as the Allocution *Singulari quadam* of 1854 (*The Christian Faith,* 813).

[37] Letter of the Holy Office to the Archbishop of Boston, 8 August 1949; Denzinger, 3866; *The Christian Faith,* 854.

> mercy, willed that their effects which are necessary to salvation can, in certain circumstances, be obtained when the helps are used only in desire or longing. We see this clearly stated in the Council of Trent about the sacrament of regeneration and about the sacrament of penance. The same, in due proportion, should be said of the Church in so far as it is a general help to salvation. To gain eternal salvation it is not always required that a person be incorporated in reality *(reapse)* as a member of the Church, but it is required that one belong to it at least in desire and longing *(voto et desiderio).* It is not always necessary that this desire be explicit, as it is with catechumens. When one is invincibly ignorant, God also accepts an implicit desire, so called because it is contained in the good disposition of soul by which a person wants his or her will to be conformed to God's will.[38]

This statement builds upon the traditional idea that the desire to be baptised is sufficient for salvation,[39] but develops it in the line of an implicit desire. Implicit desire is possible—in the line of St. Thomas—because the articles of faith are included in some most basic truths (God's existence and his providence),[40] and thus

---

[38] Letter of the Holy Office to the Archbishop of Boston, 8 August 1949; Denzinger, 3869–70; *The Christian Faith,* 855.

[39] Cf. *ST* IIIa, q.68, a.2: "The sacrament of Baptism may be wanting to anyone in reality but not in desire: for instance, when a man wishes to be baptized, but by some ill-chance he is forestalled by death before receiving Baptism. And such a man can obtain salvation without being actually baptized, on account of his desire for Baptism." It is better not to be baptized than to be baptized thanks to some sin, such as simony; cf. Thomas Aquinas, *ST* IIa IIae, q.100, a.2, ad 1: "If it were an adult in danger of death that wished to be baptized, and the priest were unwilling to baptize him without being paid, he ought, if possible, to be baptized by someone else. And if he is unable to have recourse to another, he must by no means pay a price for Baptism, and should rather die without being baptized, because for him the baptism of desire would supply the lack of the sacrament."

[40] Cf. *ST* IIa IIae, q.1, a.7: "The articles of faith stand in the same relation to the doctrine of faith, as self-evident principles to a teaching based on natural reason. Among these principles there is a certain order, so that

someone may desire implicitly baptism by being firmly attached to the more elementary truths that he already knows.[41] The object of the implicit desire is to do what is good in order to follow the divine will expressed in Providence. And the divine will is actually that human beings be saved through the incarnation, death, and resurrection of the Son of God. Therefore, people who do not know what the divine will is precisely, but try to obey it, desire unconsciously to be saved by Jesus Christ. And the community of the saved ones is the Body of Christ.

Vatican II follows the same line. It holds that membership in the Church is necessary for all who know what the Church really is, that is, for all who are not in a state of ignorance:

> This Sacred Council wishes to turn its attention firstly to the Catholic faithful. Basing itself upon Sacred Scripture and Tradition, it teaches that the Church, now sojourning on earth as an exile, is necessary for salvation. Christ, present to us in His Body, which is the Church, is the one Mediator and the unique way of salvation. In explicit terms He Himself affirmed the necessity of faith and baptism and thereby affirmed also the necessity of the Church, for through baptism as through a door men enter the Church. Whosoever, therefore, knowing that the Catholic Church

---

some are contained implicitly in others; thus all principles are reduced, as to their first principle, to this one: 'The same thing cannot be affirmed and denied at the same time,' as the Philosopher states (Metaph. iv, text. 9). In like manner all the articles are contained implicitly in certain primary matters of faith, such as God's existence, and His providence over the salvation of man, according to Heb. 11: 'He that cometh to God, must believe that He is, and is a rewarder to them that seek Him.'" Cf. IIa IIae, q.2, a.5.

[41] Cf. *ST* IIa IIae, q.2, a.5: "As regards the primary points or articles of faith, man is bound to believe them, just as he is bound to have faith; but as to other points of faith, man is not bound to believe them explicitly, but only implicitly, or to be ready to believe them, in so far as he is prepared to believe whatever is contained in the Divine Scriptures. Then alone is he bound to believe such things explicitly, when it is clear to him that they are contained in the doctrine of faith."

> was made necessary by Christ, would refuse to enter or to remain in it, could not be saved.[42]

Here again, having set forth the principle, the Council adds that those who desire to follow the divine will, but cannot identify it clearly, can also be saved:

> Those also can attain to salvation who through no fault of their own do not know the Gospel of Christ or His Church, yet sincerely seek God and moved by grace strive by their deeds to do His will as it is known to them through the dictates of conscience. Nor does Divine Providence deny the helps necessary for salvation to those who, without blame on their part, have not yet arrived at an explicit knowledge of God and with His grace strive to live a good life. Whatever good or truth is found amongst them is looked upon by the Church as a preparation for the Gospel.[43]

It is now clear that two elements must be strictly kept together, as Pope John Paul II has summarized:

> While acknowledging that God loves all people and grants them the possibility of being saved (cf. 1 Tm 2:4), the Church believes that God has established Christ as the one mediator and that she herself has been established as the universal sacrament of salvation. . . . It is necessary to keep these two truths together, namely, the real possibility of salvation in Christ for all mankind and the necessity of the Church for salvation.[44]

To put both elements together is not easy. The easiest possible errors regarding these elements are the following: to undermine the constitution of the Church in relation to Christ, or to undermine the salvific role of Christ himself, or to deny any possibility of salvation for non-Christians. It seems to me that the only way

---

[42] *Lumen Gentium,* §14.

[43] Ibid., §16.

[44] John Paul II, Encyclical *Redemptoris Missio* (7 December 1990), §9.

of avoiding all these unsatisfactory proposals is to scrutinize an ecclesiology such as St. Thomas's, in light of the contemporary understanding of the values present in other religions. Some theologians consider such a proposal unrealistic:

> We have seen that, in recent decades, there has been a shift away from the patristic and scholastic custom of giving the word "church" such a wide meaning that it included all who are being saved. The more restricted use of the term does not seek to deny the insights which the earlier usage conveyed, but rather to better serve the Church of today, with its keen awareness of the values inherent in other religions and in the world at large and its effort to work together with these others in order to realize more fully God's Kingdom.[45]

I think that, implicitly, Fr. Henn's proposal to renounce the "patristic and scholastic custom" implies choosing an ecclesiology of a Bellarminian-sociological type and limiting the salvific value of such a Church. If the Church is defined in sociological terms, as often happens after Bellarmine, then of course the religious values of other religions would have no real relation to the Church.

Some other theologians try to keep the "patristic and scholastic custom" in a different theological context. This is, for instance, is the case with the Protestant theologian Everett Ferguson. He summarizes some key points of his ecclesiology:

1. The church is where Christ is.
2. The reverse side of this is that Christ is present in the Church.
3. Christ is greater than the church.
4. Christ is the central reality of the church.

---

[45] William Henn, "The Church and the Kingdom of God," *Studia Missionalia* 46 (1997): 146.

5. There is no salvation outside of Christ.
9. Christ's presence in the world is represented by his people.
10. The church is important (Eph 1:23, 2:16, 5:23), as important as one's body is to oneself.[46]

The principles of Ferguson's ecclesiology are perfectly in line with the patristic-scholastic teaching, which is not surprising, coming from a patristics scholar. The problem of knowing how to apply such principles to the situation of non-Christians, or of baptized non-Catholics, remains.

Orthodox theologians are especially careful to avoid a division between the salvific action of Christ and his Body. They consider that Protestant and Catholic theologians have forgotten one of their own basic principles and ask a central question:

> If . . . divine grace is granted by the Church, in which the historical body of Christ is realized, then how is it possible for divine grace to be bestowed outside his body, which is the Church?[47]

Strictly speaking, Catholic theology does not say that Christ would somehow build a body of saved people outside of his Body. It rather says that the ones who most obviously belong to the Church are not the only ones who can be saved, but if others are saved, this does not happen completely without the Church:

> The universality of salvation means that it is granted not only to those who explicitly believe in Christ and have entered the Church. Since salvation is offered to all, it must be made concretely available

[46] Ferguson, *The Church of Christ,* 102–3.

[47] Vlassios Phidas, "The Limits of the Church," *The Greek Orthodox Theological Review* 38 (1993): 126. I am grateful to the *Greek Orthodox Theological Review* for having published my partial answer to the article just quoted. (cf. "A Roman Catholic Point of View about the Limits of the Church: The Article of Professor Phidas and the Roman Catholic Point of View," *The Greek Orthodox Theological Review* 42(3–4; 1997): 343–49.

> to all. But it is clear that today, as in the past, many people do not have an opportunity to come to know or accept the gospel revelation or to enter the Church. The social and cultural conditions in which they live do not permit this, and frequently they have been brought up in other religious traditions. For such people salvation in Christ is accessible by virtue of a grace which, while having a mysterious relationship to the Church, does not make them formally part of the Church but enlightens them in a way which is accommodated to their spiritual and material situation.[48]

The Congregation for the Doctrine of the Faith insists on the unity between the action of the Holy Spirit and the only economy of salvation, which is the one of Jesus Christ:

> The Church's faith teaches that the Holy Spirit, working after the resurrection of Jesus Christ, is always the Spirit of Christ sent by the Father, who works in a salvific way in Christians as well as non-Christians. It is therefore contrary to the Catholic faith to hold that the salvific action of the Holy Spirit extends beyond the one universal salvific economy of the Incarnate Word.[49]

It is not easy to hold at the same time that, Christ being the Savior, the Church has a necessary role in the salvation of all the saved, that the Church is visible, that the Holy Spirit does not build another body besides the Church, and that also some members of other religions can be saved.

This is where Cardinal Journet's principle of coextensivity of the body and soul of the Church (already mentioned) applies. Journet can avoid restricting salvation to people who are "sociologically" Christian or Catholic without denying that the Church is by nature visible:

[48] John Paul II, Encyclical *Redemptoris Missio* (7 December 1990), §10.

[49] Congregation for the Doctrine of the Faith, Notification on the book *Toward a Christian Theology of Religious Pluralism* (Maryknoll, NY: Orbis Books, 1997) by Father Jacques Dupuis, S.J. (January 24, 2001), §5, in *L'Osservatore Romano,* English edition, 14 March 2001, 16.

> Where something of the soul of the Church appears, something of her body appears. The just ones who belong to the Church by the desire of their charity, *voto, mentaliter,* without belonging yet to her totally, *re, corporaliter,* tend, without even noticing it, to exteriorize their desire. As the real meaning of this desire is still hidden from our [eyes] and their own eyes, one may say, speaking about these just, that they have an invisible membership in the visible Church.[50]

To express the same with other words: When the Holy Spirit diffuses the grace obtained by Christ, persons who accept that grace can be saved, and this has an impact on their behavior. They normally act in a charitable way, which is visible and makes them part of the visible body of Christ. Given that such persons do not appear "sociologically" to be members of the Church, Journet speaks in their case of an "invisible membership in the visible Church," that is, invisible to us because of our weak spiritual eyes. Such persons belong to the Church only in a partial way, because they have not explicitly accepted the divine covenant:

> Those who accept these uncovenanted graces are already spiritually part of the Church, but in a rudimentary, restricted fashion. All the factors in these groups that are compounded of error and sin remain outside the Church; and all they have of truth and holiness belong to her. Wherever assent is given to God by complete acceptance of his graces at a distance, the lamp of Christianity is lit. The person in question remains a Buddhist, a Jew, a Moslem or a dissident Christian; he still belongs corporally to the religious group of pre-Christian times, or to Judaism, Islam, Protestantism, but he is already spiritually of the Church. He will begin, even unawares, to act on his surroundings in order to change them; he will spontaneously stress what is authentic in them and gradually discard the rest. The Church finds in such

[50] Journet, *L'Église du Verbe Incarné,* vol. 3, 1557–58. (My translation.)

> souls hidden allies and accomplices, and begins to acquire through them, even within these alien groups, a certain visibility.[51]

That a partial Church membership can be sufficient for salvation does not mean that Christian "missions" are not necessary any more, that it is superfluous to preach the Gospel. What has already been received by these "unconscious" Christians calls for a further development. Initial graces would be better if they would become directly sacramental thanks to a kind of direct "contact" with the humanity of Christ; the persons who receive them would be more conscious and joyful if what they received were explained to them (what Journet calls "oriented" graces). Journet explains such a situation while commenting on some Muslim mystics:

> These mystics were drawn spontaneously to stress the place given in the Koran to Jesus, Son of Mary. They said that Mohammed is the greatest of the prophets, but the real saint is Jesus. They rediscovered some of the characteristics of Christian love. The reason for this we know well; Christian but uncovenanted graces crowded into their hearts. These graces may be powerful, but they are hindered from developing. If they came under the beneficent influence of the hierarchy, these graces at a distance would be succeeded by graces of contact, sacramental and orientated graces, fully "Christian" and able to make men like Christ. They would be like a rose-tree kept for a long time in an unsuitable climate which, suddenly transplanted to a sunny region, can show of what it is capable and blossom to the full.[52]

In this way, as the Church is not threatened by the truths of pagan philosophers, she is not "jealous" of the good present in other religions:

---

51 Charles Journet, *The Meaning of Grace* (New York: P. J. Kennedy & Sons, 1960), 118–19.

52 Ibid., 124.

It is impossible to say that dissidents or the unbaptized are detaining true supernatural goods that the Church does not yet possess. "Catholicism is not one religious group; it is the religion, the one true religion, and it exults without jealousy in every good, even that which is produced outside of its boundaries, for this good is outside only in appearance; in reality it belongs to the Church invisibly. Does not all, in fact, belong to us who belong to Christ!"[53]

The principles used here by Journet also apply to people who have been baptized in the Catholic Church and perhaps go on receiving sacraments, but are sinners. For Journet, our membership in the Church is never complete in this world, because we are not totally under the grace of Christ. Therefore,

The Church separates in us the good from the evil. She retains the good and leaves the evil behind. Her frontiers pass through our hearts.[54]

Journet shows that the Bellarminian approach makes it impossible to understand the relationship between the Church and salvation, both because it overestimates the "visible" membership ("visible" understood precisely in a Bellarminian way) and it underestimates the "invisible" membership (the one that for Journet is already somehow visible). This is what he says while criticizing the point of view opposite to his own:

The axiom "outside the Church no salvation" would then have stopped being universal. In order to confess the visibility of the Church in a Bellarminian way, one refuses to include charity within the definition of the Church, because it is absent in sinners

[53] Journet, *The Theology of the Church,* 218, quoting Jacques Maritain, *Religion et culture* (Paris: Desclée de Brouwer, 1930), 65.
[54] Ibid., 208.

> who are visibly in the Church and it resides in the just ones who are not visibly in the Church.[55]

Journet's ecclesiology can at the same time respect the patristic insights about the Church as Body of Christ, respect the developments about the link between the Church and salvation, take into consideration the better contemporary knowledge of the riches present in other religions, and maintain the necessity of evangelization. All of this is possible because he strictly maintains that the Church, like the human being, is both visible and invisible.

SUMMARY

St. Robert Bellarmine was a theologian of the Counter-Reformation. Suspecting that Calvin underestimated the importance of the visible Church, and wanting people to be able to know what and where the Church is, he gave a minimal definition of the Church that is limited to her sociological dimensions: a group of persons who publicly declare themselves Catholic. This limited approach was very successful: most people nowadays would understand the "Church" in a more or less Bellarminian way. But this ecclesiology is widely different from the image of the Church developed by the Fathers and the medieval theologians. From a Bellarminian perspective, or in any ecclesiology centered on canonical considerations, it is at least very difficult to understand why Aquinas could say that in a way all human beings from the beginning to the end of the world belong to the Church.[56]

Vatican II insists on the necessary union of a divine and a human element in the Church, but its texts are open to different interpretations. I suggest that a good way to understand different visions of the Church is to see, in categories common to the

[55] Charles Journet, "Regard rétrospectif. A propos du dernier livre du R. P. Congar sur l'Église," *Nova et Vetera* 38/4 (1963): 300–301.

[56] Cf. *ST* IIIa, q.8, a.3.

patristic-medieval and the Bellarminian views, how the body-soul relationship is understood.

The relation between the human soul and the human body has been understood in various ways by different philosophical systems. Most of the time, body and soul—when people do not simply deny the existence of the soul—are seen as two entities, whose combination is sometimes conflictive or hardly understandable. St. Thomas insists on the unity of both: a human being is one substance composed of body and soul.

When theologians speak about the body and soul of the Church, many of them—Catholic and Protestant—distinguish them so strongly that it is possible for people to belong only to the body or only to the soul of the Church. Visible and invisible elements can exist separately from one another, although they should be together. Applied to human beings, such a non-"psychosomatic" view would seem rather unrealistic today, and certainly contrary to the teaching of Aquinas and to the *Catechism of the Catholic Church*.[57] But, applied to the Church, the dichotomy is widely accepted.

That dichotomy between ecclesiology and anthropology is not easily accepted, if one believes with Aquinas that God relates to creatures according to their nature, according to what they are. In other words: God speaks our language so that we can understand him. Why would God relate to us in the Body of Christ in a way quite different from our unified human way of being? The first theologian to begin addressing this specific question might be Cardinal Charles Journet. For him, the body of the Church is unified by the action of her soul: the Holy Spirit acting through grace, culminating in charity. Body and soul are "coextensive"—where you have one, you have the other. Any action of the Holy Spirit received by anybody is a transmission of the salvation obtained through Jesus Christ, the only Savior, and builds the visible Body of Christ—the Church. In this way, even somebody who explicitly

---

[57] Cf. §365.

confesses a non-Christian religion, if he wants to do God's will and acts accordingly, can be in some way part of the visible Body of Christ (by the visibility of his behavior).

The ecclesiology that strictly keeps together the visible and invisible aspects of the Church helps us to understand the traditional and often misunderstood axiom *No Salvation outside the Church*. The original idea of the axiom is that Christ is the only Savior given by God to the world (being God himself), and that his action by definition builds his Body. In a Bellarminian, "sociological" ecclesiology, the axiom becomes a scandal: it seems to mean that non-Christians can never be saved, however good they might be. The Magisterium of the Church, at least since Pius IX in the nineteenth century and still at Vatican II, maintains both the necessity of Church membership and the possibility of salvation for non-Christians in a situation of invincible ignorance of Christianity. Cardinal Journet's principle of "coextensivity" systematically applies to the Church Aquinas's insights about the Church and human beings, shows how the divine-human, spiritual, and visible Church is the place of salvation also for non-Christians who want to do God's will, and does not assure salvation for unfaithful Catholics. Therefore, Catholics "can damn themselves in spite of their religion, which is true," and others "can save themselves in spite of their religion, which is wrong"[58] (at least in part).

These considerations about the Church and salvation would not be complete if a last important question were not raised: Can non-Catholic people be saved although they have another confession of faith?

[58] Charles Journet, *L'union des Églises* (Paris: Bernard Grasset, 1927), 281–82. (My translation.)

CHAPTER SEVEN

Salvation and Confession of Faith?

CHAPTER FOUR dealt with the necessity for faith to be preached by the Church. Chapter Six presented some considerations about the Church and salvation, from the point of view of Church membership. Putting together these two chapters, a last question can now be raised: Can people be saved even with different confessions of faith? This question is especially acute in the present context of plurality within Christianity, if we remember the importance of a right confession of faith for the early Church Fathers, such as St. Irenaeus (d. ca. 200):

> So, lest the like befall us, we must keep strictly, without deviation, the rule of faith, and carry out the commands of God, believing in God, and fearing Him, because He is Lord, and loving Him, because He is Father. Action, then, is preserved by faith, because unless you believe, says Isaias, *you shall not continue;* and faith is given by truth, since faith rests upon reality: for we shall believe what really is, as it is, and, believing what really is, as it is for ever, keep a firm hold on our assent to it. Since, then, it is faith that maintains our salvation, one must take great care of this sustenance, to have a true perception of reality.[1]

[1] Irenaeus, *Proof of the Apostolic Preaching,* trans. Joseph P. Smith (Westminster, MD/London: The Newman Press/Longmans, Green and Co., 1952), §3, 49.

Of course we do not believe in formulas, strictly speaking, but without them our faith cannot be expressed:

> We do not believe in formulas, but in those realities they express, which faith allows us to touch. "The believer's act [of faith] does not terminate in the propositions, but in the realities [which they express]." All the same, we do approach these realities with the help of formulations of the faith which permit us to express the faith and to hand it on, to celebrate it in community, to assimilate and live on it more and more.[2]

This chapter will address the question of the link between the profession of faith and salvation, in the context of the present divisions among Christians.

THE SIGNIFICANCE OF PARTIAL PROCLAMATIONS OF FAITH

Regarding the salvation of non-Catholics, a question applies particularly to non-Catholic Christians, who are—less than non-Christians—in a situation of invincible ignorance. Of course this is only one aspect of the question, because on the other hand if they believe in Jesus Christ, in the Trinity, if they are baptized, then they are already in a partial but very real communion with the Catholic Church. They belong to the Church much more visibly than any non-Christian. Still, Vatican II states:

> Whosoever, therefore, knowing that the Catholic Church was made necessary by Christ, would refuse to enter or to remain in it, could not be saved.[3]

The question of invincible ignorance applies to educated Christian (non-Catholic) theologians more than to anybody else. On

[2] *Catechism of the Catholic Church,* §170.
[3] *Lumen Gentium,* §14.

top of that, some questions arise from the formula of declaration of the dogmas of the Immaculate Conception and of the Assumption. In 1854, Pope Pius IX commented on his definition of the Immaculate Conception in these terms:

> If, therefore, any person shall dare to think—which God forbid—otherwise than as has been defined by us, let them clearly know that they stay condemned by their own judgment; that they have made shipwreck in their faith and fallen from the unity of the Church.[4]

In 1950, Pope Pius XII similarly said about his definition of the Assumption:

> If anyone, which God forbid, should dare wilfully to deny or to call into doubt that which we have defined, let him know that he has fallen away completely from the divine and Catholic Faith.[5]

Such texts, expressed with the highest authority of the Catholic Magisterium (in the context of a dogmatic definition, although these parts of the constitutions are not themselves part of the dogmas), could suggest that non-Catholic Christians are simply not Christian at all. The argument behind these strong expressions can be understood in the light of St. Thomas Aquinas:

> Whoever does not adhere, as to an infallible and Divine rule, to the teaching of the Church, which proceeds from the First Truth manifested in Holy Writ, has not the habit of faith, but holds that which is of faith otherwise than by faith. Even so, it is evident that a man whose mind holds a conclusion without knowing how it is proved, has not scientific knowledge, but merely an opinion about it. Now it is clear that he who adheres to the teaching of the Church, as to an infallible rule, assents to whatever the Church teaches; otherwise,

4 Pius IX, Bull *Ineffabilis Deus,* 8 December 1854; Denzinger, 2804; *The Christian Faith,* 709.

5 Pius XII, Apostolic Constitution *Munificentissimus Deus,* 1 November 1950, §45; Denzinger, 3904; *The Christian Faith,* 715.

> if, of the things taught by the Church, he holds what he chooses to hold, and rejects what he chooses to reject, he no longer adheres to the teaching of the Church as to an infallible rule, but to his own will. Hence it is evident that a heretic who obstinately disbelieves one article of faith, is not prepared to follow the teaching of the Church in all things; but if he is not obstinate, he is no longer in heresy but only in error. Therefore it is clear that such a heretic with regard to one article has no faith in the other articles, but only a kind of opinion in accordance with his own will.[6]

In the three texts just quoted, Pius IX, Pius XII, and Aquinas say the same thing: a person who does not accept one article presented by the Church as part of the faith does not have any faith at all. Aquinas explains why. A knowledge of the faith is not a philosophical knowledge; it is not something we could find out simply by thinking at length about a question. Even people who saw Jesus could not guess that he was God, although they could see him doing things that only God would have had the right to do, such as to forgive sins.[7] To recognize Jesus as God required more than human capacities; it required a revelation from God:

> When Jesus came to the region of Caesarea Philippi, he asked his disciples, "Who do people say the Son of Man is?" They replied, "Some say John the Baptist; others say Elijah; and still others, Jeremiah or one of the prophets." "But what about you?" he asked. "Who do you say I am?" Simon Peter answered, "You are the Christ, the Son of the living God." Jesus replied, "Blessed are you, Simon son of Jonah, for this was not revealed to you by man [by flesh and blood], but by my Father in heaven."[8]

The whole difference between a usual human knowledge and a knowledge of faith is that in faith the reason we say something is

---

[6] *ST* IIa IIae, q.5, a.3.

[7] Cf., for instance, Matthew 9:1–8; Luke 7:36–49.

[8] Matthew 16:13–17.

not "flesh and blood," but God. Aquinas says that if we refuse one article of faith on the basis of our own judgment, it means that our own judgment and not divine revelation is also the reason why we accept other articles of faith. It is a way of making up our own religion, a religion human and not revealed. Of course Thomas adds that divine revelation is received through the teaching of the Church: this question has already been presented in Chapter Four.

Thomas's position is not specifically Catholic. Anybody who believes in a divine revelation can see that if something is revealed by God, then that mere fact is the best reason to accept what is revealed. The principle is accepted in ecumenical dialogue, for instance by the Anglican-Roman Catholic International Commission:

> When a believer says "Amen" to Christ individually, a further dimension is always involved: an "Amen" to the faith of the Christian community. The person who receives baptism must come to know the full implication of participating in divine life within the Body of Christ. The believer's "Amen" to Christ becomes yet more complete as that person receives all that the Church, in faithfulness to the Word of God, affirms to be the authentic content of divine revelation.[9]

The question remains: How should other Christians consider what only Catholics declare to be part of divine revelation, for example, the authority of the pope, the immaculate conception, and so on?

Catholic Dogmas and the Hierarchy of Truths

In 1981, the Anglican-Roman Catholic International Commission mentioned the following question:

[9] ARCIC II, *The Gift of Authority*, §12.

> Anglicans would also ask whether, in any future union between our two Churches, they would be required to subscribe to such dogmatic statements. [for instance, the Immaculate Conception][10]

The 2004 document of the Anglican-Roman Catholic International Commission on Mary suggests a common reception or re-reception of Marian dogmas, in the light of Vatican II and of the agreement reached in the document itself.[11] This common reception does not solve completely the heart of our question: What is the situation of a non-Catholic Christian who does not accept a dogma proclaimed by the Church? Do we have to apply to him Pius XII's words and say that "he has fallen away completely from the divine and Catholic Faith?"[12] Vatican II seems to suggest a milder attitude when the Decree on Ecumenism speaks about a "hierarchy of truths." The idea is included in a paragraph that also insists on the necessity of a full presentation of Catholic doctrine:

> The way and method in which the Catholic faith is expressed should never become an obstacle to dialogue with our brethren. It is, of course, essential that the doctrine should be clearly presented in its entirety. Nothing is so foreign to the spirit of ecumenism as a false irenicism, in which the purity of Catholic doctrine suffers loss and its genuine and certain meaning is clouded. At the same time, the Catholic faith must be explained more profoundly and precisely, in such a way and in such terms as our separated brethren can also really understand. Moreover, in ecumenical dialogue, Catholic theologians standing fast by the teaching of the Church and investigating the divine mysteries with the separated brethren must proceed with love for the truth, with charity, and with humility. When com-

[10] ARCIC I, *Authority in the Church II,* §30, *Information Service* 49 (1982/II–III): 104.

[11] Cf. The Anglican-Roman Catholic International Commission (ARCIC II), *Mary, Grace and Hope in Christ,* §63, (Harrisburg, PA/London: Morehouse, 2005), 61–63.

[12] Pius XII, Apostolic Constitution *Munificentissimus Deus,* 1 November 1950, §45; Denzinger, 3904; *The Christian Faith,* 715.

> paring doctrines with one another, they should remember that in Catholic doctrine there exists an order or hierarchy of truths, since they vary in their relation to the fundamental Christian faith. Thus the way will be opened by which through fraternal rivalry all will be stirred to a deeper understanding and a clearer presentation of the unfathomable riches of Christ.[13]

The text speaks about the presentation of Catholic doctrine in a dialogue. The presentation must be complete but understandable, and therefore respectful. The "hierarchy of truths" is part of such a presentation. Does it mean that some elements of faith become secondary in such a way that they can simply be dropped? Is the Vatican II statement a complete revision of the expressions used by Pius IX and Pius XII in their dogmatic definitions?

At Vatican II, Archbishop Andrea Pangrazio of Gorizia (Italy) suggested adding the expression "hierarchy of truths":

> Even though all revealed truths must be believed with the same divine faith and all constitutive elements of the Church have to be faithfully retained, yet they are not all of the same importance.[14]

The commission that explained the text to the bishops, before they voted on the text at the Council, also mentioned that "without doubt all revealed truths must be held with the same divine faith." [15] As Pope Paul VI said during Vatican II, in his encyclical *Mysterium Fidei*:

> These formulas [that the Church used to propose the dogmas of faith] are adapted to all men of all times and all places. They can,

[13] Council Vatican II, Decree on Ecumenism, *Unitatis Redintegratio,* §11.

[14] Archbishop Andrea Pangrazio's speech to the Council, 25 November 1963, translation in Lorenz Cardinal Jaeger, *A Stand on Ecumenism: The Council's Decree* (New York: P. J. Kennedy & Sons, 1965), 115.

[15] Secretariate for Christian Unity, explanation of *modus* 49, 11 November 1964, *Acta Synodalia Sacrosancti Concilii Oecumenici Vaticani II,* vol. III.VII, 419. (My translation.)

> it is true, be made clearer and more obvious; and doing this is of great benefit. But it must always be done in such a way that they retain the meaning in which they have been used, so that with the advance of an understanding of the faith, the truth of faith will remain unchanged.[16]

A 1990 ecumenical document on the hierarchy of truths also clearly states:

> The Council's sentence does not mean that there is only a more or less incidental relationship between these truths and the foundation, so that a merely relative character stamps them, and one can consider them optional in the life of faith. Still less does the Decree's sentence consider truths of faith as more or less necessary for salvation, or suggest degrees in our obligation to believe in all that God has revealed. When one fully responds to God's self-evaluation in faith, one accepts that revelation as a whole. There is no picking and choosing of what God has revealed, because there is no picking or choosing of what revelation is—our salvation. Hence, there are no degrees in the obligation to believe all that God has revealed.[17]

The meaning of the hierarchy of truths is not to relativize anything that comes from God, but to understand it and to explain it organically. To take an example: the Immaculate Conception of Mary (defined by Pius IX in 1854) cannot be understood if Mary is not the Mother of God (as defined by the Council of Ephesus in 431), and this in turn is meaningless if Jesus is not God and man. There is then a hierarchy because some truths are more central and help one to understand the less central ones. Therefore it is wise to

[16] Cf. Paul VI, Encyclical *Mysterium Fidei*, 3 September 1965, §§24–25.

[17] Joint Working Group between the Roman Catholic Church and the World Council of Churches, *The Notion of 'Hierarchy of Truths',* An Ecumenical Interpretation, A Study Document Commissioned and Received by the Joint Working Group, Faith and Order Paper No. 150 (Geneva: WCC Publications, 1990), §25.

use such an order of exposition also in an ecumenical dialogue, since more Christians agree on the most central truths. Such a hierarchy can also be found in St. Thomas Aquinas, for whom truths can belong to faith directly or indirectly,[18] the most central ones being the ones that will be the object of beatific vision,[19] because "the chief object of faith consists in those things which we hope to see." [20] Two articles of faith are the most fundamental:

> All the articles are contained implicitly in certain primary matters of faith, such as God's existence, and His providence over the salvation of man, according to Heb. 11: "He that cometh to God, must believe that He is, and is a rewarder to them that seek Him." For the existence of God includes all that we believe to exist in God eternally, and in these our happiness consists; while belief in His providence includes all those things which God dispenses in time, for man's salvation, and which are the way to that happiness: and in this way, again, some of those articles which follow from these are contained in others: thus faith in the Redemption of mankind includes belief in the Incarnation of Christ, His Passion and so forth.[21]

In these two articles of faith, God's existence and providence, we find the root of all possible developments. How God really is

---

[18] Cf. *ST* Ia, q.32, a.4: "Anything is of faith in two ways; directly, where any truth comes to us principally as divinely taught, as the trinity and unity of God, the Incarnation of the Son, and the like; and concerning these truths a false opinion of itself involves heresy, especially if it be held obstinately. A thing is of faith, indirectly, if the denial of it involves as a consequence something against faith."

[19] Cf. *ST* IIa IIae, q.1, a.8: "To faith those things in themselves belong, the sight of which we shall enjoy in eternal life, and by which we are brought to eternal life. Now two things are proposed to us to be seen in eternal life: viz. the secret of the Godhead, to see which is to possess happiness; and the mystery of Christ's Incarnation, 'by Whom we have access' to the glory of the sons of God, according to Rm. 5:2."

[20] *ST* IIa IIae, q.1, a.6, ad 1.

[21] *ST* IIa IIae, q.1, a.7.

and what he precisely does for the world are made explicit by revelation. It is the duty of all to try to know more about these basic truths and to act according to what is known. If somebody cannot receive a more complete knowledge (in a way understandable to him), we have invincible ignorance. Something can be unintelligible for different reasons: somebody has never heard about Christianity, or identifies Christianity with the enemies of his people, or has had bad experiences with Catholic priests, and so forth. When such people do not accept what the Catholic Church proclaims as part of faith, do we have to conclude that they do not have any faith at all? Here an explanation of heresy is necessary. To be heretical means to choose to follow one's own private opinion against the teaching of the Church. But this must be conscious, because "[o]ne does not go away from the faith of the Church, except the one who knows that that from which he is moving away belongs to the faith of the Church."[22]

Only a Christian can be, strictly speaking, heretical: Members of other religions are not called "heretics" because they have never left the Church.[23] A Christian is a heretic only if he is conscious of what he is doing, because of the general moral principle already explained in the previous section. Let us apply these precisions to the central question of the present chapter: Does a Christian who refuses some articles of faith proclaimed by the Catholic Church have faith at all? For him not to have faith, he must have moved away from what he knows to be what God reveals, because the Church teaches it.

This better-formulated question includes another one: What is the relationship of a contemporary Protestant or Orthodox to the present confession of faith in the Catholic Church?

---

[22] Aquinas, *Commentary on the Sentences,* Book IV, dist. 13, q.2, a.1, ad 6 (ed. Moos, 566, n.139).

[23] Cf. ibid., Book IV, dist. 13, q.2, a.1, ad 7 (ed. Moos, 566, n.140). Cf. also *Code of Canon Law* (1983), canon 751: "Heresy is the obstinate denial or obstinate doubt after the reception of baptism of some truth which is to be believed by divine and Catholic faith."

What Is the Non-Catholic Christian's Relation to the Faith Proclaimed by the Catholic Church?

Now that preliminary points have been made clear, I can go back to the initial question of the chapter: Is it possible that Christians can be saved with a proclamation of faith different from that of the Catholic Church, having in mind that, for instance, Pius XII says that people who do not accept the dogma of the Assumption have "fallen away completely from the divine and Catholic Faith?"[24] Does what Aquinas says, that is, that "a heretic with regard to one article has no faith in the other articles,"[25] apply to all non-Catholic Christians at the beginning of the third millennium?

The point of the principle exposed by St. Thomas is simply that faith as such implies receiving revelation and not simply following our own opinions on religious questions. Most contemporary Protestant and Orthodox believers (I stress "believers") would agree with that principle. They can also have the clear will to receive divine revelation in their church, and not only on the basis of a private relationship with God. If so, they could be in a situation of ignorance, perhaps invincible for them, and they cannot be accused of heresy. Cardinal Journet summarizes their situation:

> It is of first importance to distinguish between heresy and its consequences. Heresy is the personal sin of the man who rebels against the faith by deliberately rejecting any one of the revealed truths: a personal sin can never be inherited. It is the consequences of a heresy, the legacy of a heresy, which are inherited, and which we must call a breaking away. Those who are born in these conditions will only become heretics if they deliberately make their own the original rupture. "He who defends his opinion," says St. Augustine,

24 Pius XII, Apostolic Constitution *Munificentissimus Deus,* 1 November 1950, §45; Denzinger, 3904; *The Christian Faith,* 715.

25 *ST* IIa IIae, q.5, a.3.

> "however false and perverse, without stubborn ill-will, especially when this opinion is not the outcome of pride and presumption, but when it has been inherited from parents led astray and captivated by error, if he conscientiously seeks the truth, and is ready to submit to it when he knows it, should by no means be counted as a heretic."[26]

For the time being, we can honestly speak of a real but imperfect communion among Christians. The fact that there is this real communion does not mean that the present situation of division is acceptable. It would be extreme and unjustified to consider that non-Catholic Christians are simply out of the Church and have no faith. It would also be extreme and unjustified—extremes are very similar—to accept division as a respectable fact. The ecumenical attitude of the Catholic Church is between these extremes. Pope John XXIII could develop ecumenism precisely because he insisted at the same time on a ministry of visible unity and on the value of at least some partial unity:

> We are already aware, to Our great joy, that many of the communities that are separated from the See of Blessed Peter have recently shown some inclination toward the Catholic faith and its teachings. They have manifested a high regard for this Apostolic See and an esteem which grows greater from day to day as devotion to truth overcomes earlier misconceptions. We have taken note that almost all those who are adorned with the name of Christian even though separated from Us and from one another have sought to forge bonds of unity by means of many congresses and by establishing councils. This is evidence that they are moved by an intense desire for unity of some kind.[27]

---

[26] Journet, *What is Dogma?*, 101. The internal quotation of St. Augustine is from Epist. 43, 1, quoted by St. Thomas, *ST* IIa IIae, q. 11, a. 2, ad 3.

[27] John XIII, Encyclical *Ad Petri Cathedram* (29 June 1959), §§63–64.

SUMMARY

After Chapter Four tried to show that faith must be preached, and Chapter Six presented the link between Church and salvation, Chapter Seven addresses the question about the salvation of Christians whose faith explicitly rejects some Catholic dogmas.

The importance of the question appears clearly if we consider that, for example, Pius XII, declaring in 1950 the dogma of the Assumption, said that whoever would not accept the new dogma would have "fallen away completely from the divine and Catholic Faith." [28] The reason he said this statement is to be found in Aquinas's theology of faith: Something is part of faith because the Church says that this is revealed by God (and a dogma develops the implicit content of the definitive revelation); whoever would accept or refuse any part of faith on the basis of his own opinion rather than because of the revelation transmitted by the Church would not have any faith at all, but just some philosophical ideas about religious topics. This is why Jesus praises Peter's confession of faith as different from the human points of view about Jesus' identity. Does Pius XII's statement mean that Christians who do not accept the dogma of the Assumption do not have any faith at all?

Could Vatican II's hierarchy of truths cancel Pius XII's statement, at least when applied to non-Catholics? Both Bishop Pangrazio and the commission that explained the text to the Council Fathers explicitly said that the hierarchy of truths does not mean a possibility of choosing among truths, but rather a way of seeing how different truths are related to the most central ones. For instance, Mary is the Mother of God only because Jesus is God, and she is the Immaculate Conception only because she is the Mother of God.

The necessity to accept what is revealed has been agreed upon in ecumenical dialogues, but it remains to know what is revealed. That

---

[28] Pius XII, Apostolic Constitution *Munificentissimus Deus*, 1 November 1950, §45; Denzinger, 3904; *The Christian Faith*, 715.

particular question was the subject of Chapter Four. Non-Catholic Christians who want to accept what God reveals to them cannot be accused of substituting divine authority with the idol of their private opinion, and thus they cannot be accused of having lost any faith because they do not accept one or more Catholic dogmas. If Catholic ecumenism implies presenting the fullness of doctrine, so that unity can be possible, it does not imply at all denying any presence of truth or faith in other Christian denominations. Quite the opposite: these shared truths are the basis of the dialogue.

CHAPTER EIGHT

General Conclusion

AS ANCIENT PHILOSOPHERS had already noticed, everyone strives for happiness, and supreme happiness is beyond our finite reach. Human beings are therefore a paradox: among living beings that we can observe in nature, we are the only ones who cannot be satisfied by less than an infinite knowledge, love, and happiness, and therefore we are the only sensitive beings that seem misplaced in this world. In other words, our nature seems to be made for the infinite, which is God.

My purpose here is not to argue for the existence of God (although I plan to write another book on the question). I just assume that there is a God. This book aims at presenting to believers and to unbelievers how Catholics find an answer to the basic human quest for happiness, for a meaningful human life.

How does God look at this pitiful creature whose soul is too big for the clothes of this world? St. Thomas Aquinas says that if God would not give us a way to fulfil the desires of our nature, there would be some mistake by the Creator himself, which is impossible.[1] But it seems impossible for a finite being to fulfil his infinite desire by his own capacities. Therefore, one can expect, if

---

[1] Cf. Aquinas, *Sententia libri Ethicorum,* Book 1, lectio 2, nr.3.

God exists, that he reveals himself. Christians believe that God has actually revealed himself in his Son Jesus Christ, who is himself the one God made man. Christ our Savior grants us not only some knowledge about God, but the possibility to be eternally with God, even to take part in divine life. And this salvation respects our human social nature: we are saved within a community, which is the Body of Christ, the People of God, the Church.

As our salvation is not limited to some time or place, the Church lasts as long as Christ's salvation: for ever, first in this world, then in Heaven (although the Church in Heaven does not keep all features of the Church in this world). This is proclaimed in every Eucharist: The whole Church praises God; we Christians on earth sing with the angels and the saints in Heaven. For the time being, in this world, the Church must have some way of staying with Christ, with his saving grace, with his teaching. If that were impossible, how could divine revelation be of any use to us? Of course God knows this, and he provided us with human ministers so that we would not soon destroy his divine gifts. In order that the Church would not disappear at his Ascension, Jesus Christ left his apostles in charge of diffusing his good news. With Christ's authority, the apostles could even decide which observances of the Old Testament would be kept. The apostolic community completed the Bible, writing in and for the living Church the New Testament, whose authors are the Holy Spirit and human writers, working together at two different levels in a way that respects the mode proper to each. Correct metaphysical distinctions of the levels of beings and of causes make it possible to avoid both fundamentalism and biblical liberalism. In order that the Church would not disappear at their death, the apostles left in their place certain successors: the bishops, who continue the part of the apostolic ministry that is permanently necessary.

So that his good news could be known, Christ decided to send preachers. Salvation is offered to human beings by human means. Such a trust in human beings is an amazing sign of divine love. But, as human beings sometimes make mistakes, how can we know after two millennia that what is preached to us today is still Christ's message? The question is made acute by the divisions among Christians: Can we and should we choose between the sometimes divergent Christian ways? Different interpretations of the Bible will always occur, as well as different understandings of the Church, and the best exegetical and historical tools cannot solve all the differences. Aquinas and his theological school say that God has provided us with a permanent and—on the main points—infallible help within our human condition: the teaching of the Church, part of the episcopal ministry unified by the communion with the successor of Peter. Without such a ministry our knowledge of God would never be sure, and therefore divine revelation would be useless. Without such a ministry Christian unity would be forever impossible: Who would have the authority to say that henceforth previously-divided Christians are one, and will stay one? Without such a ministry ecumenism would simply become pointless or desperate. This clear authority is the contribution of Catholic dogma—dogma as a permanently necessary feature of the Church until the end of time—to ecumenism.

Preaching is not enough for people to receive faith. One must recognize as true what is proclaimed. These are for Aquinas the two conditions of faith. What is preached—by human means but coming from God—can be accepted as true only with divine grace. Divine grace makes possible our human free decision to accept revelation, although it leaves us the possibility to refuse it. God does not act only in the individual believers, but also in the ministry: ministers have fully human acts (as the writers of the Bible), but these acts can transmit grace only because God is also active in them. Both God and the minister do the same act, at the same time, at two different levels. The relation between these acts can be compared to the relation between my act and the act of my pen when I write: two simultaneous acts, both complete at their level, with the difference that a human being, unlike a pen, is free.

The aforesaid may give the impression of an overestimation of the Church. Part of such a suspicion comes from a sociological understanding of the Church, in which she is seen as a specific group of human beings, limited in many ways. That idea is due to the influence of some Counter-Reformation theologians, like St. Robert Bellarmine. Medieval theologians did not see the Church mainly at a sociological level: they saw her as the impact of Christ's grace in human lives. As this grace is offered to all, Thomas Aquinas could say that, somehow, all human beings of all times belong to the Church, because all are at least invited to salvation. Such a view of the Church does not exclude its visibility, which the Bellarminian view wanted to highlight. Cardinal Journet follows and develops St. Thomas's views on the Church: the Church has both a body and a soul (the Holy Spirit acting through our charity), and they are "coextensive" in the Church as they are in human beings, because when he relates to us God respects our human nature. Whoever accepts the divine invitation starts belonging to the Church, and that membership is not totally invisible because the behavior of the person changes: the body of the Church starts being present. This Thomistic ecclesiology makes it possible to understand what is meant by "No salvation outside the Church": "to be in the Church" and "to be saved" mean the same thing, because to be in the Church means to be under the salvific influence of the Head of the Church, that is, Jesus Christ. The real spiritual goods, wherever they are, belong to Christ and to his Body. When such a membership is not complete (in different degrees, which is the case for all non-Catholics and all Catholic sinners), it must become more complete, so that what is good may grow and flourish.

Full membership in the Church implies the profession of the apostolic faith. To have faith means to receive certain truths because they are revealed by God in and through the Church. Any other way of accepting or refusing revealed truths, for example the content of the Creed, is not faith, but just a personal opinion founded not on divine authority, but on personal judgement: faith is then substituted by a philosophy of religion. For this reason, when Pius XII proclaimed the dogma of the Assumption in 1950, he said that whoever would refuse the dogma would have "fallen away completely from the divine and Catholic Faith." This teaching does not seem easily compatible with ecumenical dialogue. Did Vatican II change such a teaching when it spoke about a hierarchy of truths? It was explained at the Council itself and in a later ecumenical dialogue that the hierarchy of truths does not allow for a choice among revealed truths, but that all revealed truths do not have the same place in the organic complex of the revelation centered on Jesus Christ. A dialogue on faith must have Jesus Christ as its starting point and then proceed to understand how other truths are related to the center. It is indispensable for every Christian to receive revelation from God in joyful and grateful obedience, and this revelation is not given to isolated individuals. Although ignorance can be culpable, it is also possible for someone to ignore without guilt that God has entrusted his revelation to the Church, whose fullness is in the Catholic Church: an invincible ignorance cannot be condemned, but all should do their best to avoid ignorance.

Anyone who carefully looks at human life can see that human beings desire something infinite. The dynamism of knowledge and of love shows that much. God, who has made us in this way, does not abandon us. He reveals himself in his Son, so that we can even participate in his life, without end. But God does not reveal himself to human beings without respecting our human nature because, as Aquinas says in a basic axiom, "it belongs to Divine providence to provide for each one according as its condition requires." [2] God

[2] *ST* IIIa, q.61, a.1. Cf. some texts already quoted: "God moves everything in its own manner. . . . Hence He moves man to justice according to the condition of his human nature" (*ST* Ia IIae, q.113, a.3); "It is proper to an instrument to be moved by the principal agent, yet diversely, according to the property of its nature" (*ST* IIIa, q.18, a.1, ad 2).

speaks to us in human "terms," first of all in the Incarnation, but also in the consequences of the Incarnation. As in creation itself—in which God "has wished to communicate His likeness to creatures, not only in point of their being, but likewise in point of their being causes of other things" [3] and "God so governs things that He makes some of them to be causes of others in government; as a master, who not only imparts knowledge to his pupils, but gives also the faculty of teaching others"[4]—so too in redemption God even associates the Church in his salvific work. For this reason Jesus gathers a community, a structured community, that goes on until the end of time. God acts fully for our salvation, but he associates with his work active human "instruments": the Church. As human beings are visible (by their body) and have an invisible soul, and since God respects human nature in his dealings with us, the Church then is inseparably visible and invisible. Any saving act of God at least starts building the body of his Church.

At times, the Church is an occasion of scandals. But she is above all a sign of the immense love of our God who respects us so deeply, scandalous as we are. He loves us so much that he chooses to entrust to us not only the care of ourselves and each other, but even the transmission of himself in his own Divine Word.

---

[3] *Summa contra Gentiles,* Book III, chap. 70.

[4] *ST* Ia, q.103, a.6.

BIBLIOGRAPHY

THE BIBLE is not indicated in the bibliography. The biblical texts are usually quoted according to the New International Version, except when another translation seemed more appropriate.

ABBREVIATIONS

Ia	Thomas Aquinas, *Summa theologiae* Prima Pars
Ia IIae	Thomas Aquinas, *Summa theologiae* First part of the Secunda Pars
IIa IIae	Thomas Aquinas, *Summa theologiae* Second part of the Secunda Pars
IIIa	Thomas Aquinas, *Summa theologiae* Tertia Pars
Montreal 1963	Faith and Order, *The Fourth World Conference on Faith and Order, Montreal 1963*

TEXTS OF THE MAGISTERIUM OF THE CHURCH

The English translations of all Vatican II texts, all papal texts (with their respective paragraph numbers), the *Code of Canon Law*, the *Catechism of the Catholic Church,* have been taken from www.vatican.va, except when indicated differently.

In some cases, the references are given to the Denzinger (i.e., Heinrich Denzinger, *Enchiridion symbolorum definitionum et declarationum de rebus fidei et morum,* paragraph numbers of any edition published since 1963) and to *The Christian Faith* [Jacques Dupuis ed., Sixth Revised and Enlarged Edition (New York: Alba House, 1996), quoted by paragraph numbers].

Boniface VIII, Bull *Unam Sanctam,* 18 November 1302; Denzinger, 870 and 875; *The Christian Faith,* 804.

Congregation for the Doctrine of the Faith, Notification on the book *Toward a Christian Theology of Religious Pluralism* (Maryknoll, NY: Orbis Books, 1997) by Father Jacques Dupuis, S.J. (January 24, 2001), §5, *Osservatore Romano,* English edition, 14 March 2001, 16.

———, *The Message of Fatima,* Theological Commentary, 26 June 2000, *Osservatore Romano,* English edition, 28 June 2000.

Council of Florence, *Decree for the Copts,* 4 February 1442; Denzinger, 1351; *The Christian Faith,* 810.

Council Vatican I, Dogmatic Constitution on the Catholic Faith, *Dei Filius,* Introduction, *Decrees of the Ecumenical Councils*: Trent to Vatican II, edited by Norman P. Tanner S.J.; original text established by G. Alberigo [et al.], London: Sheed and Ward, 1990, vol. 2.

———, Dogmatic Constitution on the Church, *Pastor Aeternus,* Introduction, *Decrees of the Ecumenical Councils,* vol. 2.

Council Vatican II, *Acta Synodalia Sacrosancti Concilii Oecumenici Vaticani II,* Rome: Typis Polyglottis Vaticanis, 1970–78 (volumes of the sessions themselves).

———, Decree on Ecumenism, *Unitatis Redintegratio,* 21 November 1964.

———, Dogmatic Constitution on Divine Revelation, *Dei Verbum,* 18 November 1965.

———, Dogmatic Constitution on the Church, *Lumen Gentium,* 21 November 1964.

John XIII, Encyclical *Ad Petri Cathedram,* 29 June 1959.

John Paul II, Encyclical *Ecclesia de Eucharistia,* 17 April 2003.

———, Encyclical *Redemptoris Missio,* 7 December 1990.

———, Encyclical *Ut Unum Sint,* 25 May 1995.
Holy Office, Letter to the Archbishop of Boston, 8 August 1949; Denzinger, 3866–69; *The Christian Faith,* 854–55.
Paul VI, Encyclical *Ecclesiam Suam,* 6 August 1964.
———, General Audience, 22 January 1964, *Osservatore Romano,* Edizione quotidiane italiana, 23 January 1964, 1
———, Encyclical *Mysterium Fidei,* 3 September 1965.
Pius IX, Allocution *Singulari quadam,* 1854, *The Christian Faith,* 813.
———, Bull *Ineffabilis Deus,* 8 December 1854; Denzinger, 2804; *The Christian Faith,* 709.
———, Encyclical *Quanto Conficiamur Moerore,* 10 August 1863; Denzinger 2865–67; *The Christian Faith,* 814.
Pius XII, Apostolic Constitution *Munificentissimus Deus,* 1 November 1950; Denzinger, 3904; *The Christian Faith,* 715.
———, Encyclical *Humani Generis,* 12 August 1950.

Classical texts

I mean by "classical" all texts published before 1700. Medieval authors are referred to with the Christian name (e.g., Thomas Aquinas), while more recent authors are referred to with the surname (e.g., Luther, Martin).

The translation of the quoted Latin texts has been sometimes modified without warning, for the sake of precision.

Aristotle, *De Anima.* Translated by J. A. Smith, taken from classics.mit.edu/Aristotle/soul.2.ii.html.
———, *Nicomachean Ethics,* translated by W. D. Ross, Oxford: Clarendon Press, 1906.
Augustine, *Contra Epistulam Fundamenti,* Corpus Scriptorum Ecclesiasticorum Latinorum 25 (Sect. VI, Pars I), Prag/Vienna/Leipzig: Tempsky-Freitag, 1891.
———, *Enarrationes in Psalmos,* LI-C, Corpus Christianorum Series Latina 39, Turnhout: Brepols, 1956.
Bellarmine, Robert, *De Controversiis Christianae Fidei Adversus Hujus Temporis Haereticos,* II, lib.3, De Ecclesia militante, caput II, translations

taken from John A. Hardon, *A Comparative Study of Bellarmine's Doctrine of the Relation of Sincere Non-Catholics to the Catholic Church,* Rome: Excerpta ex dissertatione . . . , Pontificia Universitas Gregoriana, 1951.

Bonaventura, *Breviloquium,* in *Opera omnia,* vol. V, Quaracchi: Ex Typographia Collegii S. Bonaventurae, 1891, 199–291.

———, *Commentarius in Evangelium Joannis,* in *Opera omnia,* vol. VI, Quaracchi: Ex Typographia Collegii S. Bonaventurae, 1893, 237–532.

Bossuet, Jacques-Bénigne, *Histoire des variations des Églises protestantes,* 2 tomes, Paris: Chez la Veuve de Sébastien Mabre-Cramoisy, Imprimeur du Roy, 1688.

Cajetan [Thomas De Vio], *In Summ. Theol.,* IIa IIae, q.1, a.1, in Sancti Thomae Aquinatis Doctoris Angelici *Opera omnia,* Iussu impensaque Leonis XIII P. M. edita, vol. 8, Rome: Ex Typographia Polyglotta S. C. De Propaganda Fide, 1895, 5.

Calvin, John, *Catechism of the Church of Geneva,* translation from www.reformed.org/documents.

———, *Institutes of the Christian Religion,* Philadelphia/London: The Westminster Press/S.C.M. Press, 1967 (4).

Cyprian, *Letters* (1–81), translated by Sr. Rose Bernard Donna, C.S.J., "The Fathers of the Church," Washington, DC: The Catholic University of America Press, 1964; original: Corpus Christianorum Series Latina III B-C, Turnhout: Brepols, 1994–96.

Ioannes a Sancto Thoma, *Cursus theologicus,* In Summam theologicam D. Thomae, Nova editio, Tomus primus, Vivès, Paris, 1883, and Tomus septimus, 1886.

Irenaeus, *Proof of the Apostolic Preaching,* translated by Joseph P. Smith, Westminster/Maryland/London: The Newman Press/Longmans, Green and Co., 1952.

Jurieu, Pierre, *Le vrai système de l'Église et la véritable Analyse de la foi,* Où sont dissipées toutes les illusions que les controversistes Modernes, Prétendus Catholiques, ont voulu faire au public sur la Nature de l'Église, son Infaillibilité et le Juge des Controverses, Chez la Veuve de Caspar et chez Théodore Goris, Dordrecht: Chez la Veuve de Caspar et chez Théodore Goris, 1686.

Luther, Martin, *The Bondage of the Will* (*De servo arbitrio,* 1525), in

Luther's Works, vol. 33, Philadelphia: Fortress Press, 1972.

Plato, *Alcibiades*, translation by Sanderson Beck taken from san.beck.org/Alcibiades.html.

———, *Phaedo*, translation by Benjamin Jowett taken from classics.mit.edu/Plato/phaedo.html.

———, *Symposium*, translation by Benjamin Jowett taken from www.gutenberg.org/etext/1600.

Thomas Aquinas, *Commentary on John (Lectura Super Ioannem)*, R. Cai ed., Turin: Marietti, 1952.

———, *Commentary on the Psalms (In Psalmos Davidi Expositio)*, in *Sancti Thomae Aquinatis Opera Omnia*, tomus XIV, Parma: Typis Petri Fiaccadori, 1863.

———, *Commentary of the Sentences (Scriptum Super Sententiis)*, Book IV, ed. M. F. Moos, Paris: Lethielleux, 1947.

———, *Compendium theologiae*, in *Sancti Thomae de Aquino Opera Omnia*, Iussu Leonis XIII P. M. edita, vol. 42, Rome: Editori di San Tommaso, 1979.

———, *De Malo*, translation from *The De Malo of Thomas Aquinas*, With Facing-page Translation by Richard Regan, Edited with and Introduction and Notes by Brian Davies, Oxford/New York: Oxford University Press, 2001.

———, *De Veritate*, translation from St. Thomas Aquinas, *Truth*, translated by Robert W. Mulligan, James V. McGlynn, and Robert W. Schmidt, Chicago: Henry Regnery Company, 1952–54.

———, *Sententia libri Ethicorum*, in *Sancti Thomae de Aquino Opera Omnia*, Iussu Leonis XIII P. M. edita, vol. 47/I–II, Rome: Editori di San Tommaso, 1969.

———, *Summa contra Gentiles*, literally translated by the English Dominican Fathers from the latest Leonine edition, London: Burns Oates & Washbourne, 1923–24.

———, *Summa theologiae*, published under the title: *Summa theologica*, translated by Fathers of the English Dominican Province, London: R. & T. Washbourne, 1911–35.

———, *Super Boethii De Trinitate*, in *Sancti Thomae de Aquino Opera Omnia*, Iussu Leonis XIII P. M. edita, vol. 50, Rome-Paris: Cerf, 1992.

ECUMENICAL TEXTS

This section contains texts published by different kinds of ecumenical commissions.

Anglican-Roman Catholic International Commission (ARCIC I), *Authority in the Church II,* in *Information Service* 49, 1982/II–III, 98–105.

———, (ARCIC II), *Mary, Grace and Hope in Christ,* Harrisburg, PA/London: Morehouse, 2005.

———, (ARCIC II), *The Gift of Authority*: Authority in the Church III, An agreed statement by the [second] Anglican-Roman Catholic International Commission, London: CTS, 1999.

Faith and Order, *A Treasure in Earthen Vessels,* An instrument for an ecumenical reflection on hermeneutics, Faith and Order Paper, No. 182, Geneva: WCC Publications, 1998.

———, *Confessing the One Faith,* An Ecumenical Explication of the Apostolic Faith as it is Confessed in the Nicene-Constantinopolitan Creed (381), New Revised Version, Faith and Order Paper, No. 153, Geneva: WCC Publications, 1991.

———, *The Fourth World Conference on Faith and Order, Montreal 1963,* edited by P. C. Rodger, Executive Secretary, Commission on Faith and Order, World Council of Churches, and Lukas Vischer, Research Secretary, Commission on Faith and Order, World Council of Churches, New York: Association Press, 1964.

———, *Towards Sharing the One Faith,* A Study Guide for Discussion Groups, Faith and Order Paper No. 173, Geneva: WCC Publications, 1996.

Groupe des Dombes, *"Un seul maître,"* L'autorité doctrinale dans l'Église, Paris: Bayard, 2005.

Joint Working Group between the Roman Catholic Church and the World Council of Churches, *The Notion of 'Hierarchy of Truths,'* An Ecumenical Interpretation, A Study Document Commissioned and Received by the Joint Working Group, Faith and Order Paper, No. 150, Geneva: WCC Publications, 1990.

Other Works

Bea, Augustine, *The Way to Unity after the Council,* London: Geoffrey Chapman, 1967.

Congar, Yves M.-J., *Esquisses du mystère de l'Église,* Paris: Cerf, 1953.

Ferguson, Everett, *The Church of Christ: A Biblical Ecclesiology for Today,* Grand Rapids, MI/Cambridge: W. B. Eerdmans, 1996.

Henn, William, "The Church and the Kingdom of God," *Studia Missionalia* 46 (1997): 119–47.

Hick, John, *The Rainbow of Faiths,* Critical dialogues on religious pluralism, London: SCM, 1995.

Jaeger, Lorenz, *A Stand on Ecumenism: The Council's Decree,* New York: P. J. Kennedy & Sons, 1965.

Journet, Charles, *L'Église du Verbe Incarné,* vol. 2, Saint-Maurice: ed. Saint-Augustin, 1999.

———, *L'Église du Verbe Incarné,* vol. 3, Saint-Maurice: ed. Saint-Augustin, 2000 (second part of vol. 2 in the 1951 edition).

———, *L'union des Église,* Paris: Bernard Grasset, 1927.

———, *The Meaning of Grace,* New York: P. J. Kennedy & Sons, 1960.

———, "Regard rétrospectif. A propos du dernier livre du R. P. Congar sur l'Église," *Nova et Vetera* XXXVIII/4 (1963): 294–312.

———, *The Theology of the Church,* translated by Victor Szczurek, San Francisco: Ignatius Press, 2004.

———, *What is dogma?,* London: Burns & Oates, 1964.

Lindbeck, George A., *The Future of Roman Catholic Theology: Vatican II—catalyst for change,* Philadelphia: Fortress Press, 1970.

Möhler, Johann Adam, *Unity in the Church or The Principle of Catholicism,* Presented in the Spirit of the Church Fathers of the First Three Centuries, Washington DC: The Catholic University of America Press, 1996.

Morerod, Charles, "A Roman Catholic Point of View about the Limits of the Church: The Article of Professor Phidas and the Roman Catholic Point of View," *The Greek Orthodox Theological Review* 42 (3–4); 1997): 343–49.

Newman, John Henry, *Certain Difficulties Felt by Anglicans in Catholic Teaching,* In a Letter addressed to the Rev. E. B. Pusey, D.D., on occasion of his Eirenicon of 1864; And in a Letter addressed to the

Duke of Norfolk, on occasion of Mr. Gladstone's Expostulation of 1874, Vol. II, new impression, London, New York and Bombay: Green, and Co., 1900.

Phidas, Vlassios, "The Limits of the Church," *The Greek Orthodox Theological Review* 38 (1993): 119–29.

Pottmeyer, Hermann J., art. "Bischof," *Lexikon für Theologie und Kirche,* Bd.2, Freiburg im Br.: Herder, 1994 (3), col. 484–85.

Ratzinger, Joseph, "Discorso in apertura del Simposio," in *Il primato del successore di Pietro,* Atti del Simposio teologico, Roma, dicembre 1996, "Atti e Documenti" 7, Roma: Libreria Editrice Vaticana, 1998, 17–18.

———, " 'Teologia sapienzale'. Sollecitudine di Giovanni Paolo II per il terzo millenio," in *Fede di studioso e obbedienza di pastore,* Atti del Convegno sul 50° del Dottorato di K. Wojtyla e del 20° del Pontificato di Giovanni Paolo II, a cura di Edward Kaczynski, Roma: Millennium Romae, 1999, 77–88.

Schopenhauer, Arthur, "Preischrift über die Grundlage der Moral," §2, in *Sämtliche Werke,* Bd. 4, Leipzig: Brockhaus, 1938.

Soloviev, Vladimir, *La Russie et l'Église universelle,* in *La Sophia et les autres écrits français,* Lausanne: La Cité—L'Age d'Homme, 1978 (French original text).

Sullivan, Francis A., *Salvation outside the Church? Tracing the History of the Catholic Response,* London: Geoffrey Chapman, 1992.

Zizioulas (Metropolitan John of Pergamon), "Primacy in the Church: An Orthodox Approach," in James F. Puglisi, S.A., editor, *Petrine Ministry and the Unity of the Church: Toward a Patient and Fraternal Dialogue,* Collegeville, MN: Michael Glazier, The Liturgical Press, 1999, 115–25.

GENERAL INDEX

INDEX OF SCRIPTURAL CITATIONS